To:. . . . .

From: . . . .

Date:. . . . .

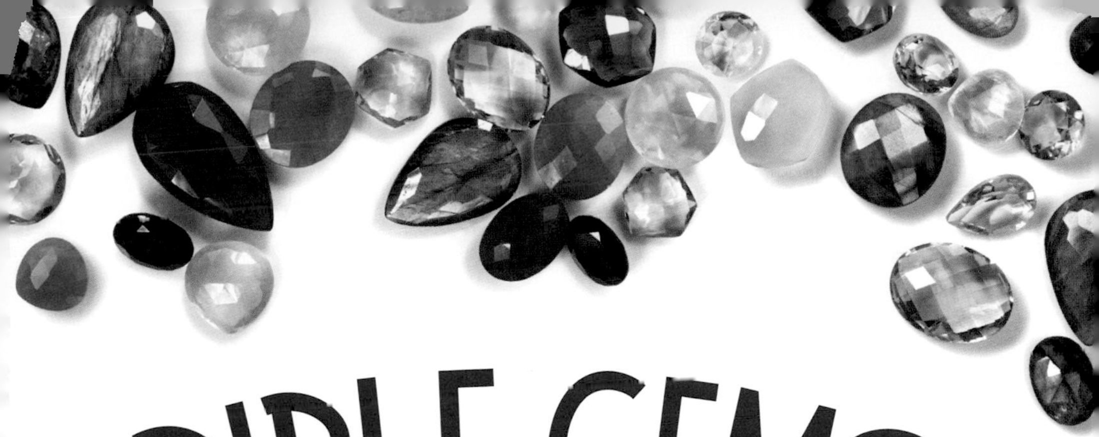

BIBLE GEMS
–TO–
REMEMBER

DEVOTIONS FOR KIDS

52 Devotions with Easy Bible
Memory in 5 Words or Less

ROBIN SCHMITT

ZONDERKIDZ

Bible Gems to Remember Devotions for Kids
Copyright © 2019 by Robin Schmitt

Requests for information should be addressed to:
Zonderkidz, 3900 Sparks Dr. SE, Grand Rapids, Michigan 49546

ISBN 978-0-310-74625-6 (softcover)

ISBN 978-0-310-74773-4 (ebook)

Interior design: Denise Froehlich
Interior photos: from iStock, Shutterstock, and 123RF

Printed in China

19 20 21 22 23 /DSC/ 10 9 8 7 6 5 4 3 2 1

DEDICATION

This book is dedicated to my wife, Helen, in honor of all she has done through the years to bring God's Word to his children.

—RS

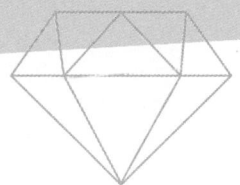

ACKNOWLEDGMENTS

I would like to express my appreciation to: Kim Childress and Barbara Herndon for seeing the potential of Gemstones and helping others at Zondervan see it too; Andrea Vinley Converse and Mary Hassinger for their editorial expertise; Joe McCarthy for his wise counsel, support, and prayers; and my many brothers and sisters in Christ who encouraged me and prayed for me as I wrote this book. Thanks to all of you!

There is a mine for silver
and a place where gold is refined.
Iron is taken from the earth,
and copper is smelted from ore.
But where can wisdom be found?

—JOB 28:1–2, 12

TABLE OF CONTENTS

A NOTE TO PARENTS

Bible Gems or Gemstones are very short, very powerful clauses from the Bible. They are no more than five words long, so they are easy to remember. Children can memorize them instantly. A Gemstone is a nugget of truth mined from Scripture. Here's an example:

The LORD is good.

This book offers a year's worth of inspiring, encouraging Gems—one per week—paired with insightful devotions to help readers understand the Gem and relate to it. Children will learn 52 pocket-sized truths from God's Word, truths they can carry with them forever. Plus, there are more than 100 extra Gems that complement the main Gemstones.

Learning what the Bible says and putting it into practice is one of the best means to build character and faith. With that in mind, here are five ways children and their families can use the Gemstones in this book:

1. Memorize them.
2. Think about them.
3. Talk about them.
4. Pray about them.
5. Live them out.

The idea of using Bible Gems to help children treasure God's Word in their minds and hearts was inspired in part by the apostle Paul. In 1 Corinthians 14:19, Paul wrote about speaking five clear words of instruction. Can you imagine what he would say in five words or less to teach children a valuable truth? Perhaps something like this:

Do everything in love. —1 CORINTHIANS 16:14

I pray that God will enable children, and the adults who love them, to grasp the truths in these Gemstones and remember them forever, and that the beauty of these Gems will inspire everyone to dig deeper into God's Word.

—ROBIN SCHMITT

1 THERE IS A GOD.

1 Samuel 17:46

David said to [Goliath], "You come against me with sword and spear and javelin, but I come against you in the name of the Lord Almighty, the God of the armies of Israel, whom you have defied. This day the Lord will deliver you into my hands . . . and the whole world will know that there is a God in Israel."
—1 Samuel 17:45–46

Goliath was a big man, and he was strong. Everyone was in awe of him, both friends and enemies. He was popular with his fellow soldiers and feared by everyone else. He was wealthy too; one look at all his glittering armor proved that. His king richly rewarded him as the best fighter for the Philistines.

Yes, Goliath was quite a guy. But he didn't really have it all together. He may have been good at throwing that heavy javelin of his. He probably won a lot of javelin-tossing contests. But in one important matter, he totally missed the bull's-eye.

Some people, by their words and actions, show that they don't believe in God. They talk and act as if God doesn't exist.

They tell themselves, "There is no God," and they act like it's true.

Goliath was that kind of guy. He didn't believe the biggest truth of all. He may have believed in *other* gods, but he didn't believe in the Lord—the one, true, living God. And that is simply foolish (Psalm 14:1). It's sad to say, but Goliath denied God and paid for it when he insulted God and God's army.

Other people, by what they say and do, prove that they believe in God. They *know* God is real, because they know God. They have a relationship with him. They've heard his voice, they've felt his presence, and they've experienced his power. They don't have to wonder if God exists, because God is right there with them.

David was like that. He knew God well—God had helped him kill lions and bears when they attacked his sheep (1 Samuel 17:34–37). David told a giant, two armies, and the whole world that God was real. Then he proved it by defeating Goliath with the Lord's help. A young man with a slingshot conquers a huge, invincible warrior—solid evidence that God exists!

"There is a God in heaven who reveals mysteries."

Daniel was another guy with faith. He stood before the king of Babylon—the richest, most powerful man in the world—and said, "There is a God." His exact words were, "There is a God in heaven who reveals mysteries" (Daniel 2:28). Then Daniel proved his claim by telling what the king had dreamed and what it meant. God had shown it all to

Daniel, and sure enough, everything in the king's dream came true—more evidence that God is real.

People like Goliath often talk others into adopting their foolish beliefs. Many people looked up to Goliath—and not just because he was tall. When someone you look up to says, "There is no God," don't buy it. Turn to people like David, Daniel, and other heroes of the Bible, and get a second opinion.

Be confident in your faith in God, and pray for people who don't believe in him. Encourage your skeptical friends to try looking for God. If they honestly and earnestly do, they'll find him.

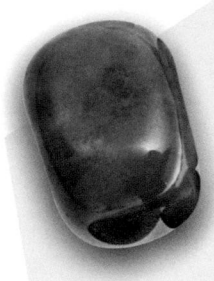

MORE GEMS

Believe in God.
—ACTS 16:34

He exists.
—HEBREWS 11:6

2 THE LORD IS GOOD.

Psalm 100:5

The Lord is good and his love endures forever;
his faithfulness continues through all generations.
—Psalm 100:5

Psalm 34:8 says, "Taste and see that the Lord is good." It's a simple principle, really. Like when you go to the ice cream shop and there's a new flavor. You'll never know if it's good unless you ask for a sample. Then they hand you one of those little plastic spoons, and you try it.

In other words, you need to get to know God. Not just by reading about him in the Bible (although that's a great place to begin) but also by talking with him in prayer and walking with him in life. You have to experience God for yourself.

As soon as you start getting to know God, you start learning the truth about him. And the truth is, he is good. The Bible puts it this way: "God is light; in him there is no darkness at all" (1 John 1:5). Isn't that a great image? God isn't just halfway decent; he is pure goodness, through and through! There's no shadow of evil in him.

Psalm 100:5 points out two aspects of God's goodness: God is loving, and God is faithful. Love and faithfulness are in God's nature, part of who he is deep down. So "his love endures forever," and "his faithfulness continues through all generations." God will always love you and keep his promises to you. Why? Because God never changes. And that's another good thing about him!

Isn't it wonderful to know that God—the all-powerful King who rules over everything in heaven and on earth—is good? Remembering this truth gives Christians great comfort, because God has promised that no matter what happens in this world, he will use it for good (see Romans 8:28).

Should one little taste of God's goodness be enough to convince you that God is always good, all the time? In a way, yes, because God is so good that just one taste can give you the faith to trust in him completely. But don't stop with a tiny sample and toss your little plastic spoon. Grab a big spoon and dig in. Keep getting to know God better. The more you do, the more you'll understand how truly good he is. Your faith will grow deeper, and you'll be more and more sure of his goodness.

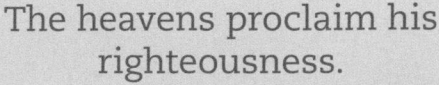

MORE GEMS

God is righteous.
—DANIEL 9:14

The heavens proclaim his
righteousness.
—PSALM 97:6

3 GOD LOVES YOU.

Deuteronomy 23:5

[The LORD] tends his flock like a shepherd:
He gathers the lambs in his arms
and carries them close to his heart.
                    —ISAIAH 40:11

Have you ever used an analogy, or a "word picture," to describe something? Maybe you saw a bright light in the sky one night and the next day you told your friend it was like a really big star or a streak of lightning.

The Bible uses many analogies to show us how much God loves us. It says God is like a father who has compassion on his children. Or like a mother who comforts her child. Or like an eagle hovering over its young, catching them when they fall and carrying them on its mighty wings.

Maybe the best way the Bible shows us God's love is by describing him as a shepherd. Psalm 23 says that God is like a shepherd who watches over us, provides for us, guides us, and comforts us. When a person wanders away from God because of his sins, God searches for him like a shepherd looking for the sheep he loves. And when God finds him, he carries that person home on his shoulders (Luke 15:3–6).

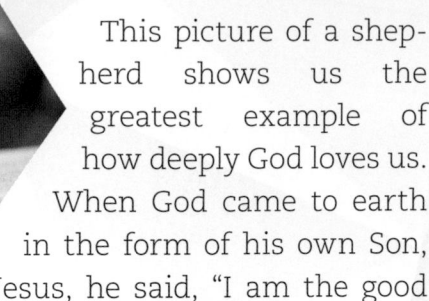

This picture of a shepherd shows us the greatest example of how deeply God loves us. When God came to earth in the form of his own Son, Jesus, he said, "I am the good shepherd. The good shepherd lays down his life for the sheep" (John 10:11). A good shepherd doesn't run away when a wolf attacks his flock. He is willing to die to save his sheep. God loves us so much that he was willing to die for us to save us from our sins.

Long ago, God told his people, "I have loved you with an everlasting love" (Jeremiah 31:3). And he has proved his love in so many ways! Day by day, God continues to watch over you, provide for you, guide you, and comfort you. And if you ever wander away from him and get lost, he'll come rescue you. Knowing that God is such a good shepherd, you can praise him like King David did, saying, "Great is your love toward me" (Psalm 86:13).

MORE GEMS

The Father himself loves you.
—JOHN 16:27

The LORD is my shepherd.
—PSALM 23:1

4. WE ARE GOD'S HANDIWORK.

Ephesians 2:10

We are God's handiwork, created in Christ Jesus to do good works, which God prepared in advance for us to do.

—Ephesians 2:10

In Rome, Italy, is a building called the Sistine Chapel. This chapel is famous because of its beautiful ceiling, painted more than 500 years ago by a man named Michelangelo. Since he was such a talented artist, he was chosen to decorate the chapel's ceiling. Michelangelo had to paint while standing on a wooden scaffold over sixty feet above the floor. It took him four years to finish his masterpiece.

When Michelangelo began painting the ceiling of the Sistine Chapel, he didn't just wake up one morning, pick up his paintbrush, climb onto the scaffold, and start doodling. No, a great artist puts a lot of thought into what he wants to create. Every grand work of art begins with a vision—something the artist "sees" or imagines.

Michelangelo's mural shows many scenes from the Bible, including the classic image of God creating Adam. Looking at it today, you can see the careful planning Michelangelo put

into his work. He was a master artist who focused on every detail. From the beginning, he had something amazing in mind. He also had the skill to design it and create it.

God had an awesome vision in mind when he made the first human being. And he had an awesome vision in mind when he made you. According to the Bible, God envisioned you even before the world began. He's been thinking about you for a long time.

God is not only the greatest artist ever; he also has the greatest mind. Don't forget, he wrote all the laws of science! And God has the ability to create whatever he imagines. With all of his wisdom and power, God did a magnificent thing when he made you. But he's not done with you yet.

Philippians 1:6 says, "He who began a good work in you will carry it on to completion." God has a great plan for who you will be and what your life will become.

Also, God made you for a purpose—so you could do great things. You see, you're not the only one God has been thinking about this whole time. God has a vision for this world too, and all the people in it.

God had an awesome vision in mind when he made the first human being.

Can you imagine the kinds of things God made you to do to help others? Maybe he wants you to invent stuff that will make other people's lives safer or easier or better. Maybe he wants you to become a doctor so you can help people get well. Maybe he wants you to be a police officer so you can protect people. Or maybe he wants you to create beautiful artwork to inspire people and point them toward him.

As you're growing up, God is teaching you and training you, getting you even more ready for the great things he wants you to accomplish. There's important work to be done, and God is shaping you into the right person for the job.

God, the greatest artist of all, envisioned you, designed you, and created you. You're his masterpiece—handmade and treasured. And he made you for a reason. Right from the start, you've been a part of his vision for the world.

MORE GEMS

God created human beings.
—DEUTERONOMY 4:32

You created my inmost being.
—PSALM 139:13

Your works are wonderful.
—PSALM 139:14

5 CHRIST HAS SET US FREE.

Galatians 5:1

It is for freedom that Christ has set us free. Stand firm, then, and do not let yourselves be burdened again by a yoke of slavery.

—GALATIANS 5:1

Have you ever seen a bird trapped in a garage? Some garages have windows on the walls, and when a bird flies inside, it often will flutter around one of the windows. The blue sky beyond the clear glass pane makes the bird think the window is a way out. It sure looks like the path to freedom! So the bird keeps flying into the glass instead of turning and escaping easily out the big, wide-open garage door.

Many people live trapped too. They're not really happy where they are, but they think they know how to get to a better place. The problem is, their attempt to get free isn't taking them anywhere. They keep banging into a dead end. And the whole time, they never see the wide-open door right beside them.

For example, Sarah envies Lindsey, one of her classmates, because Lindsey's family has lots of money. Lindsey lives in a big house, she wears nice clothes, and her mom drives her to

He is the door to freedom.

school in a cool car. Her family eats at fancy restaurants all the time. They also own a cottage and a boat, and they spend every weekend at the lake. Lindsey always talks about all the fun activities she gets to do and the awesome places she gets to go. It drives Sarah crazy! In fact, it bothers Sarah so much that she's trapped in jealousy.

So how does Sarah deal with it? Well, there are a couple of "windows" she keeps flying into. For one thing, she treats

Lindsey badly. Every time they interact, Sarah speaks rudely to her, and she never invites Lindsey to do anything or offers to help her in any way. (Lindsey struggles with her schoolwork sometimes, and she could use some help.) Sarah thinks acting like this will make her feel better, but it really doesn't. It kind of gives her a headache.

For another thing, Sarah tries to "keep up" with Lindsey. She begs her parents for money to buy trendy clothes, and she complains when they don't eat out much. Sarah is always comparing her life to Lindsey's. She dreams of living in a bigger house and going on fun trips, and keeps hoping it'll all happen soon. She's trying to make herself feel better, but she ends up feeling sad.

The only way Sarah can escape this trap is to turn to Jesus. He is the door to freedom. In John 14:6, Jesus said, "I am the way." He was telling his disciples that he was the only way to their heavenly Father—which also means Jesus is the only way to true liberty. If Jesus sets you free, you will really be free (see John 8:36). Jesus would show Sarah that "godliness with contentment is great gain" (1 Timothy 6:6), and she would find joy in the life God gave her. She could get rid of all her jealousy and start treating Lindsey with love. And Sarah would find herself out in the sunny blue sky, soaring free.

If you ever get trapped, remember the true way out. Don't keep flying into windows. Turn to Jesus and experience real freedom. Then *stay* free—don't fly back into the garage!

MORE GEMS

You have been set free.
—ROMANS 6:18

Live as free people.
—1 PETER 2:16

6 GOD WILL BE WITH YOU.

Joshua 1:9

*Be strong and courageous. Do not be afraid; do not be discouraged, for the L*ORD *your God will be with you wherever you go.*

—JOSHUA 1:9

There are scary times when it's good to know God is around. Like when you're away from your parents and the tornado sirens go off, and everyone has to take cover. Or when you get separated from your family on vacation, and you're lost in a city or forest. Times like these make you glad that God promised to stay with you and watch over you.

Sometimes it's tough situations that make you grateful for God's presence. Like when you're taking an important test and the questions are hard. Or when you run into that kid down the street who's kind of a bully, and you're not sure what to say or do. You start to panic, but then you remember you're not alone. God is beside you, ready to help you, guide you, and protect you.

The children living in Judah during the time of King Jehoshaphat faced a *very* scary situation. (See 2 Chronicles 20:1–22.) A huge army was coming to attack Judah, and all the

God is with you now, and he'll be with you your whole life.

people—men, women, and children—gathered to ask God for help. God's Spirit came on a man in the crowd, and the man told everyone not to be afraid, that God was with them and would fight the battle for them. Sure enough, the next day God—"the Mighty Warrior who saves" (Zephaniah 3:17)—set ambushes that defeated the enemy army.

Psalm 46:11 says, "The LORD Almighty is with us." Those are encouraging words! You don't have to be afraid. You don't have to face this great big world all by yourself. Your powerful heavenly Father is always near.

You're growing up every day. Before long, you'll be in high school, driving a car, taking yourself everywhere you need to go. And someday you'll be a young adult, moving out of your parents' house and striking out on your own. At that point, you won't need your parents to watch over you anymore. But you'll never outgrow your need for God.

God doesn't want you to outgrow him. You were never designed for that kind of independence. In fact, God wants you to depend on him more and more as you get older. He wants you to become more aware of his presence each day, and put more trust in his promises. That's a big part of what growing up spiritually is all about.

Knowing that God is with you now, while you are young, builds your faith and courage so you can face all the situations that come your way: the next-big-step ones, the sudden-big-crisis ones, and the everyday-problem ones.

God is with you now, and he'll be with you your whole life. That's really good to know today, and it's really good to remember down the road. So remind yourself when you're feeling alone and scared. God has promised to be with you always, and he's always faithful to his promises. He won't leave you for a second.

MORE GEMS

God is with us.
ISAIAH 8:10

He will never leave you.
DEUTERONOMY 31:6

I will not be afraid.
PSALM 118:6

7 DO WHAT IT SAYS.

James 1:22

Do not merely listen to the word, and so deceive yourselves. Do what it says.
—JAMES 1:22

When your parents are driving somewhere you haven't been before, do they use a phone or GPS to help them figure out how to get there? It's pretty cool! You just enter the address you're looking for, and a map pops up. Then a voice tells you where to go. The technology is very useful, and it's fun to watch your progress on the map as you travel along.

But having all that guidance wouldn't do much good if your parents didn't follow the directions. What if your mother kept going straight when the voice said to turn? Or she turned left when the voice told her to turn right? You'd probably shout, "Mom, where are you going?"

Today's gadgets are so advanced, they would keep figuring out new routes. But if all your mom did was listen to the voice talking and never obeyed what it was saying, you'd never reach your destination. You wouldn't end up where you wanted to go.

The Bible is a lot like that. (It will even reroute you when you get off course!) James wrote that it's possible to fool yourself by reading or listening to God's Word but not using it in your life. You think you're okay because you know a lot of Bible stories and maybe even memorized some Bible verses. But it's not really helping you much, because it hasn't affected the way you treat other people or the way you live.

That's why this Gemstone—"Do what it says"—is one of the most important ones in the Bible. If you carry this one in your pocket, it will remind you to practice many other Gemstones from God's Word.

When you look at commands like "Love one another," "Encourage one another," "Pray for each other," "Forgive one another," and "Serve one another," you won't just think, *Those are nice ideas.* You'll make an effort, with God's help, to love, encourage, pray for, forgive, and serve people around you. And that will make all the difference in your world.

Jesus said something similar to "Do what it says." He put it this way: "Everyone who hears these words of mine and *puts them into practice* is like a wise man who built his house on the rock. . . . But everyone who hears these words of mine and does not put them into practice is like a foolish man who

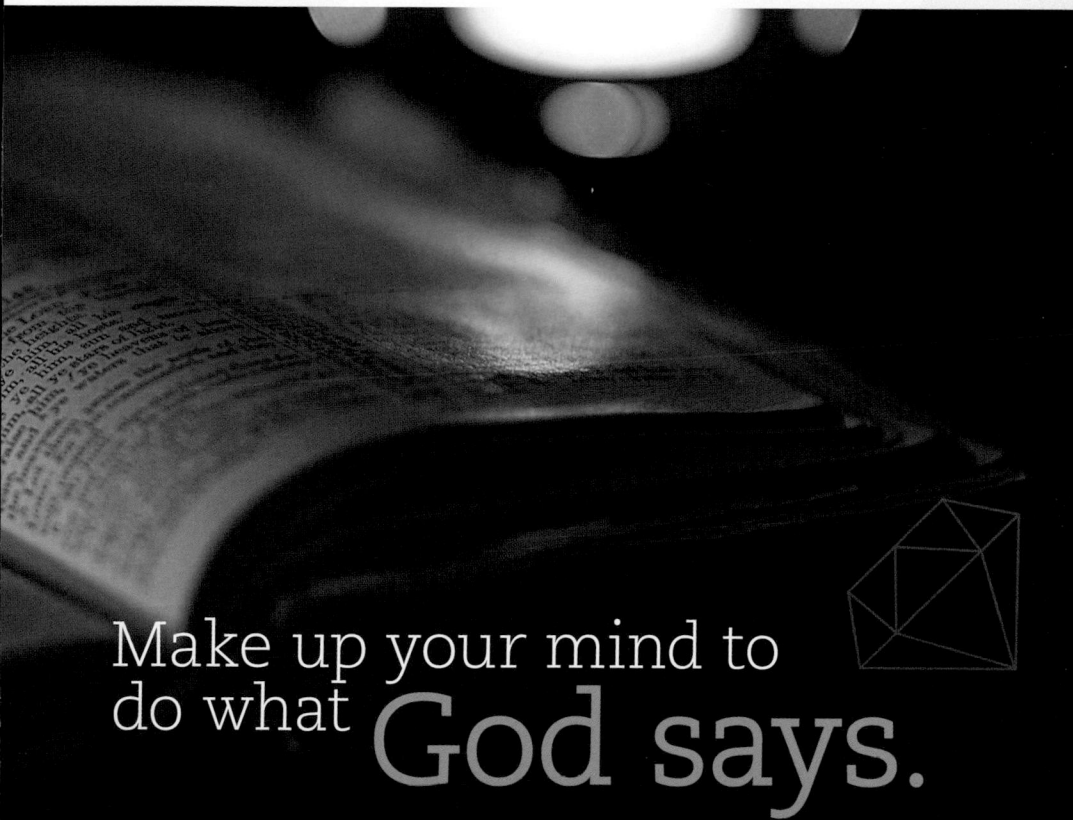

Make up your mind to do what God says.

built his house on sand" (Matthew 7:24, 26, emphasis added). Which house do you think would hold up better? Which one would you rather live in?

It's great to study the Bible, memorize Scripture verses, think about what they mean, and talk about them with others. And it's wonderful to paste them all over your locker or make posters out of them and hang them in your bedroom. But this isn't enough.

Make up your mind to do what God says. Decide to put Jesus's words into practice. When you combine God's commands with faithful obedience, you'll experience the power of God's Word in your life.

MORE GEMS

Obey the LORD's commands.
—JUDGES 3:4

Put them into practice.
—MATTHEW 7:26

Listen and obey.
—DEUTERONOMY 5:27

8 JESUS LIVES FOREVER.

Hebrews 7:24

Because Jesus lives forever, he has a permanent priesthood. Therefore he is able to save completely those who come to God through him, because he always lives to intercede for them.
—Hebrews 7:24–25

Sometimes in a great story, the hero dies at the end. Just when things look hopeless, he gives his own life to save everyone else. The people are so grateful, but they also feel sad. Yes, they're alive. But their beloved hero is gone, never to return.

Along with sadness comes fear. Who will rescue them next time? The hero saved this day—but what about tomorrow?

Can you imagine how the disciples felt when Jesus died on the cross? They didn't realize what a heroic thing he had done. To them, their beloved leader had been arrested and put to death. Jesus seemed weak and helpless. His disciples didn't know he was the most powerful being on earth and could have called an army of angels to help him if he chose. The disciples didn't get it that Jesus had sacrificed himself

He had died to save them—
and now he was alive!

in order to save people like them—sinners who really were helpless in the face of God's righteousness.

The disciples had put all their hope in Jesus. They were convinced that he was the one God had sent to rescue their people from the Romans who ruled over them. Instead, the Romans crucified Jesus. It was the worst possible ending to the story. The hero was dead, and no one was saved.

But then something astounding happened. Jesus showed up again! God brought him back to life.

Jesus proved it was true by showing his disciples the nail marks in his hands and feet and even eating with them. He explained why he had to die and be raised from the dead. Finally the disciples understood, and suddenly their sadness turned to rock-solid hope. Jesus really was the hero they needed. He had died to save them—and now he was alive! The story couldn't have turned out better.

Think about what all this means. Jesus came back to life just days after he was crucified. He is still alive today. And he will go on living forever. The bad guy in this story, our enemy Satan, took his best shot at Jesus. Jesus was already killed, and he conquered death! Now nothing can touch him. Jesus is invincible. Our hero will never die again.

Jesus made the ultimate sacrifice to save the world. So in one sense, his job as a hero is finished. His death was enough to rescue everyone who believes in him. It will never need to be repeated. But in another sense, Jesus's work as a hero continues. The Bible says he lives forever to stand before God and defend every sinner who has faith in him. And God gladly forgives us. After all, it was his plan all along.

Jesus has one more heroic deed to accomplish. One day, in true hero fashion, he is going to ride in on a great white horse for a final rescue mission. (See the book of Revelation!) Actually, Jesus will come back for two reasons. He'll return to take his rightful place as King of this world. And he'll gather up his faithful followers to spend eternity with him in heaven.

Because our hero lives forever, we'll live forever too!

MORE GEMS

My redeemer lives.
—JOB 19:25

He is able to save.
—HEBREWS 7:25

He will save his people.
—MATTHEW 1:21

9 LIVE FOR THE LORD.

Romans 14:8

Whatever you do, do it all for the glory of God.
—1 CORINTHIANS 10:31

Make a poster showing all the things that matter to you. Draw a big, round target, and put symbols for them on the rings of the target. The more important something is, the closer it should be to the middle. And the most important one of all needs to go right in the bull's-eye.

What will you draw on your poster? Where will you put them on the target? And what will be in the center?

Now ask yourself, "What am I living for?" People live for all kinds of things. Some people live for weekends and vacations. You can live for clothes and jewelry. You can live for food. You can live for sports and hobbies. Or movies, TV, and video games. Or thrills and adventure. Or music, writing, and art. In other words, what do you focus on the most? What gives your life purpose and meaning? Why do you do what you do each day?

With all these choices, what does God say to live for? Live for him! This doesn't mean you have to become a monk or a nun, or erase everything from your poster and write "God" across the whole target. But it does mean that God should be what's most important in your life.

God doesn't want to take away everything you care about in this world. But he does want to be the one thing you care about most. If you live for him, he'll use everything in your life to build his kingdom, draw others to him, and bring him glory.

Look at how God used some important stuff in people's lives because they were living for him: David moved from leading and caring for sheep to leading and caring for God's people. Peter went from catching fish to fishing for men and women and making them disciples. Mary worked hard around the home she grew up in, hoping to be a mom one day; she became the mother of Jesus. Joseph liked building things out of wood; his carpentry skills helped him earn a living and raise God's Son.

Put God in the center of your universe. Dedicate everything you care about to him, trusting in his plans for you. Focus on him, obey him, serve him. Living for God is the best way to live. It gives purpose and meaning to everything else.

MORE GEMS

Seek first his kingdom.
—MATTHEW 6:33

Serve him with all faithfulness.
—JOSHUA 24:14

10 GOD IS FAITHFUL.

1 Corinthians 10:13

*The LORD is trustworthy in all he promises and
faithful in all he does.*
—PSALM 145:13

Has anyone ever promised to do something great for you and then didn't? If so, you were probably very disappointed.

On the other hand, have you ever known someone who always keeps promises? That's a person you can trust and believe.

Imagine how the Israelite leaders felt when Joshua reminded them of God's faithfulness. By this time, God had rescued his people from slavery in Egypt, led them far across the desert, brought them into the Promised Land, and helped them defeat their enemies so they could live at peace in their new country. Joshua was an old man now, and he wanted to make sure that the Israelites would remember how trustworthy God was.

So Joshua summoned the leaders and spoke to them. "You yourselves have seen everything the LORD your God has done," he said (Joshua 23:3). "You know with all your heart and soul that not one of all the good promises the LORD your God gave you has failed. Every promise has been fulfilled" (v. 14).

What a statement! God had kept every single promise he

had ever made to them. The leaders had seen it for themselves. The evidence was all around them; they were standing victorious in the land God promised them. They knew deep down they could always trust God. Their hearts and souls must have overflowed with hope!

Why not do something to remind yourself of God's faithfulness? Samuel set up a stone as a reminder that God faithfully helped his people (see 1 Samuel 7:12). You could start a stone collection to remind you of times when God helped you. Find some stones, and use a permanent marker to write a few words on each one about a way God has helped you. Keep the stones in a jar where you can see them. Then

Every promise has been fulfilled.

add to your collection every time God helps you. The stones will inspire you to keep trusting God.

It's not always easy to trust God, because life gets scary sometimes. We have to learn to take our eyes off anything that makes us afraid and to focus on the One who gives us hope. As the author of the book of Hebrews says, "Let us hold unswervingly to the hope we profess, for he who promised is faithful" (Hebrews 10:23).

MORE GEMS

The Lord is trustworthy.
—Psalm 145:13

Great is your faithfulness.
—Lamentations 3:23

11 THERE IS ONLY ONE GOD.

Romans 3:30

There is but one God, the Father, from whom all things came and for whom we live.
—1 CORINTHIANS 8:6

Many people wonder about whether God exists, who he is, and which god to believe in. But there was no doubt in Elijah's mind. He knew two very important things: there is a God, and there is only *one* God.

Elijah was a prophet, and he was convinced that the Lord was the one true God. But many prophets in Elijah's time served a false god named Baal. They were leading the people of Israel to follow Baal instead of the Lord. So Elijah challenged these prophets to a contest. It was a whose-God-can-make-fire competition.

They held the contest on Mount Carmel. There, the prophets of Baal did their best to get Baal to start a fire. They shouted and danced. Then they shouted louder and danced harder, trying to get a response from Baal.

Nothing.

Finally, it was Elijah's turn. He said a simple prayer, not much more than, "LORD, the God of Abraham, Isaac and

Israel, let it be known today that you are God" (1 Kings 18:36). Immediately, fire came down from heaven!

The people of Israel fell to the ground and began crying out, "The LORD—he is God! The LORD—he is God!" Now they were convinced.

How about you? Are you convinced that the God of the Bible is the one, true, living God? Are you persuaded that he is the only God who has ever existed, the only God there is, the only one there ever will be?

The Bible is full of evidence proving that God is who he claims to be. There are stories about God healing people, feeding them, protecting them, and rescuing them—in amazing, miraculous ways. If you still have some doubt, keep reading these stories. They will build up your faith.

And the evidence doesn't stop there. In the 2,000 years since Bible times ended, God has done many astounding things—and he is still performing miracles today. Study science, read church history, and talk to others who have experienced God's power. Tune in to the great things he is doing in people's lives. Ask God to reveal himself to you. Like Elijah and the people of Israel, you'll come to realize that the Lord alone is God.

MORE GEMS

You alone, LORD, are God.
—2 KINGS 19:19

There is none like you.
—PSALM 86:8

12 NOT MY WILL, BUT YOURS.

Luke 22:42

Jesus went out as usual to the Mount of Olives, and his disciples followed him. . . . He withdrew about a stone's throw beyond them, knelt down and prayed, "Father, if you are willing, take this cup from me; yet not my will, but yours be done."

—LUKE 22:39, 41–42

Do you know what a motto is? It's a favorite saying that someone chooses to live by. It becomes a guiding principle. "Carpe diem!" is one—it's Latin for "Seize the day!" Other popular mottoes are "Practice makes perfect" and "Laughter is the best medicine."

Some people choose a favorite Bible quotation as their motto—except they call it their "life verse." They memorize it, carry it in their heart, and live by it.

If Jesus had a motto, it was probably "Not my will, but yours." Those were the words he lived by. He spoke them as he prayed to his heavenly Father, and he put them into practice. We could even think of this as Jesus's Gemstone, the powerful little truth he carried around in his pocket.

Jesus once told his followers, "I have come down from

Not my will, but yours.

heaven not to do my will but to do the will of him who sent me" (John 6:38). And another time, he said, "I always do what pleases him" (John 8:29).

Jesus made up his mind right from the start to obey his Father at all times and do what God wanted him to do. And he followed through with that decision right to the end, when he fulfilled the mission God gave him—to die on the cross for the sins of the world.

How about making Jesus's motto your motto? When you follow this guiding principle, you're following in the footsteps of Christ.

What about when you have a hard time doing God's will? Jesus knows what that's like. In the garden of Gethsemane, before he was arrested, Jesus was struggling mightily as he prayed. He didn't want to suffer and die on the cross (he compared it to drinking a cup of something very bitter), and he asked his Father not to make him do it. When Jesus said, "Not my will, but yours," he was submitting to his Father's will. But he was also letting go of what he wanted and grabbing hold of what his Father wanted. Jesus knew that through his suffering and death, God was going to redeem the world.

Slip this Gemstone into your pocket, knowing that what

God wants is always best. Keep studying the Bible so you'll "understand what the Lord's will is" (Ephesians 5:17). The more you know about God's will, the more you'll realize how good and wonderful it is. You'll always be better off when you trade your desires for what God desires for you.

MORE GEMS

Obey the LORD.
—DEUTERONOMY 27:10

Listen and obey.
—DEUTERONOMY 5:27

Seek God's will.
—EXODUS 18:15

13 LOVE THE LORD.

Mark 12:30

Love the Lord your God with all your heart and with all your soul and with all your mind and with all your strength.

—MARK 12:30

Could you sum up all the rules in the Bible in five words? Jesus did, in a way. A man challenged him to name God's most important command. Jesus replied that the most important one was to love the Lord with everything in you. Then he added that the second most important one was to love your neighbor as yourself. Everything in the Scriptures, Jesus said, boiled down to these two commands. In five words, they are:

Love God, and love people.

So how do we obey God's most important command?

Isn't love just a feeling? You either love pizza or you don't. You're either passionate about puppies or you're not. How can there be a command to love?

First of all, Jesus was talking about a higher kind of love than the way you might feel about pizza and puppies. This love isn't merely a noun; it's also a verb. It's not just something you feel; it's also something you do.

Jesus said we need to love God with our heart, but also with our soul, mind, and strength. Love for God is about feeling emotion for him *and* using our physical energy to serve him. That means praying to him, worshiping him, doing good deeds, and telling others about him.

Will you choose to love God? Here's the real secret: God is worthy of all the love you can give! The more you get to know him, the more deeply you'll love him. As you learn about God and spend time with him, you'll understand how good and wise and wonderful he is.

When you realize how much God loves you and how much he has done for you, you can't help but love him back. God wants to be the love of your life. That's the motive behind his number one command. And if you make him your first love, he will help you love others in your heart and in your actions. That's the secret behind his number two command.

With all the rules in the Bible, what does God really want from us? It's simple. He wants us to love him, and he wants us to love each other.

MORE GEMS

I love you, LORD.
—PSALM 18:1

My spirit longs for you.
—ISAIAH 26:9

14 THE LAST WILL BE FIRST.

Matthew 20:16

[Jesus asked his disciples], "What were you arguing about on the road?" But they kept quiet because on the way they had argued about who was the greatest.

Sitting down, Jesus called the Twelve and said, "Anyone who wants to be first must be the very last, and the servant of all."

—MARK 9:33–35

As a young boxer, Cassius Clay—later known as Muhammad Ali—kept bragging, "I am the greatest!" And to prove it, he challenged the world's heavyweight champion, Sonny Liston. So in 1964, the two men got in a ring to fight each other and show everyone who was supreme.

Today boxers still climb into a ring to battle each other for the right to call themselves number one. And all kinds of people, in all kinds of places, argue and struggle with each other to be the one on top. Things haven't changed much since 1964. And they haven't changed much since Jesus was here.

Jesus must have grown tired of people fighting about who was the greatest. Can you imagine? He was the King of Kings,

Humble

the Son of God—the greatest person who ever lived. But so many others were trying to prove that they deserved the most honor.

It even happened one day when a man invited Jesus over for a meal. Many other guests were there, and Jesus watched them scramble for the most important places at the table. It was like a game of musical chairs! So Jesus tried to teach them a valuable lesson. "When you go to a wedding feast," he said, "don't rush to grab the special seats up front. Someone more important may have been invited, and you'll be embarrassed when the host asks you to move. You'll have to take a seat in the back. Instead, sit in the back when you arrive. Then the host will say, 'Come and sit closer to me,' and you'll be honored in front of everyone."

The guests all wondered what Jesus meant. So he spelled it out. "If you raise yourself up, God will humble you. But if you humble yourself, God will raise you up." (See Luke 14:7–11.)

On another occasion, Jesus's disciples were arguing about which of them was the greatest. Once again, he offered worthy advice. "If you really want to be number one, act like the least important person of all, and serve everybody else." (See Mark 9:33–35.)

Would you believe that at the Last Supper, the disciples argued again about who was the most important? During the meal, Jesus demonstrated what he was talking about. The greatest person who ever lived rose from the table, picked up

ourself and serve others.

a wash basin and towel, got down on his knees, and washed his disciples' feet.

They were shocked! He said, "You call me your Lord and Teacher. That's right; that's who I am. And now that I've served you, you should serve one another. I've set an example for you, and you'll be blessed if you follow it." (See John 13:1–17 and Luke 22:24–27.)

Have you ever wanted to be the greatest? Do you want to feel important? That's okay! Jesus didn't scold his disciples for wanting to be great. He simply told them—and then showed them—the right way to do it.

The way to be great is not to brag about yourself or push your way to the front of the line—or even knock someone out in a boxing ring. If you want to be great, follow Jesus's example. Humble yourself and serve others.

MORE GEMS

Be the very last.
—MARK 9:35

Take the lowest place.
—LUKE 14:10

Serve one another humbly.
—GALATIANS 5:13

 **DO EVERYTHING IN LOVE.**

1 Corinthians 16:14

Love is patient, love is kind. It does not envy, it does not boast, it is not proud. It does not dishonor others, it is not self-seeking, it is not easily angered, it keeps no record of wrongs. Love does not delight in evil but rejoices with the truth. It always protects, always trusts, always hopes, always perseveres. Love never fails.

—1 CORINTHIANS 13:4–8

If you look closely at a diamond, you'll see that it has many facets. These are the tiny surfaces the stonecutter made while shaping the rough mineral into a polished jewel. The facets reflect light at many angles, making the diamond sparkle. They also split up the light like little prisms, making beautiful colors. Each facet shows a different part of the same precious gem.

Reading the Scripture passage above is like gazing at the facets of love. Take a close look at them again.

Sixteen different aspects of love are described. They tell you what love is like and show you how to follow God's second-greatest command. God first wants us to love him, of

love shines as beautiful as a diamond.

course. That's his greatest command. But he also wants us to love others—or, as the apostle Paul put it, to "do everything in love."

This passage proves that love isn't some misty thing that's hard to grasp. It's as solid as a diamond. Each facet of love mentioned here is something real you can put into practice. And when you do, love shines as beautiful as a diamond.

For example, let's say it's field day at school, and you and a bunch of kids are playing soccer. How do you put love into practice then? Do you run around smiling, praising God in your heart for butterflies, and trying to love everyone around you?

Well, there's nothing wrong with that. But what happens when one of the kids on your team loses the ball, and the other team scores? You could get annoyed and scowl. Or say something mean. If you really want to do things in love, though, you might say something encouraging to your teammate. Because showing kindness is a facet of love.

What if someone passes the ball to you, and you kick it in the net for a goal? How do you love God and others now? Do you drop to one knee, point to heaven, and think loving thoughts toward people everywhere?

Nothing wrong with that either. But what happens when you get home and your little brother wants to tell you about something cool he did that day? Maybe you ignore him and brag about your own accomplishment. But if you really want to do things in love, you might listen to his story and praise him for what he did. Because being humble and honoring others are facets of love.

If it helps you remember what love is all about, you can break up the principles in 1 Corinthians 13:4–8 into short gems: "Love is patient," "Love is kind," "Love is humble," "Love honors others" . . . You get the idea! Make a poster out of them, or flashcards. Then try to learn them all. Or challenge yourself to memorize the whole passage, just as it's written.

When you do things in love, you'll be thinking about others. You'll be putting their wants and needs before your own. You'll be following Jesus's example by treating people the way he would. And you'll be pleasing God.

MORE GEMS

Love your neighbor.
—LEVITICUS 19:18

Foster love.
—PROVERBS 17:9

Follow the way of love.
—I CORINTHIANS 14:1

16 TRAIN YOURSELF TO BE GODLY.

1 Timothy 4:7

Train yourself to be godly. For physical training is of some value, but godliness has value for all things, holding promise for both the present life and the life to come.

—1 TIMOTHY 4:7–8

When you're learning to play a guitar, you have to train your fingers. First, you have to learn where to put them to make a chord. Then you have to learn how to hold down the strings properly so they make a nice, clean sound when you strum them. And then you have to learn how to move your fingers quickly to make different chords so you can play songs.

It takes a lot of mental effort, because you have to memorize the patterns that make up the chords. And it takes a lot of physical effort, because you have to practice for hours to make your fingers strong and flexible. You must work hard and keep at it, trusting that you *will* make progress.

Also you have to endure a little pain. There's no way

around it—learning to play guitar hurts a bit. Your hands get sore from stretching your fingers, and your fingertips get sore from pushing on the strings.

So is it worth it?

The answer is yes! Anyone who loves to play guitar will tell you that all the effort and suffering pays off. The long hours of practice empower you to make music, and it's very rewarding.

Training has great value, not only for musicians but also for athletes, artists, architects, and astronauts. Everyone goes through a certain amount of training in order to do the things they want to do. But the most valuable training of all is the kind that teaches you to be godly. This training helps you grow spiritually. It teaches you how to live the way God wants you to live. It makes you more like him, so you start to think the way he thinks and see the world the way he does. This training gives you the same

the most valuable training of all is the kind that teaches you to be godly.

character qualities God has—such as kindness, goodness, faithfulness, gentleness, and self-control. Spiritual training enables you to reject what is wrong and embrace what is right. It empowers you to love people the way God does.

Just like learning to play guitar, training yourself to be godly takes mental and physical effort. You have to learn what to do by reading the Bible, paying attention at church, and listening to godly people in your life. Then you have to practice what you've learned. You must work hard, be patient, and never give up. It's not easy, but it's worth it. You'll surely grow in godliness, because God guarantees it!

And yes, there will be some pain along the way. It hurts a bit to stop being selfish and start putting other people first. It's kind of painful to forgive someone who's done something bad to you. It hurts a little to give away some of your allowance or a box of clothes or toys to someone in need.

But all that effort and suffering pays off big-time. That's God's promise. And he's a great Coach who will help you train yourself to be like him. Listen to God, trust him, and practice everything he tells you. It will be amazingly rewarding. Your mind will be filled with wisdom, your heart will be filled with love, and your hands will acquire the skill to do so much good in this world. Like a well-trained musician playing great songs on a guitar, you'll make beautiful music with your life.

MORE GEMS

Live holy and godly lives.
—2 PETER 3:11

Follow God's example.
—EPHESIANS 5:1

Be holy.
—1 PETER 1:15

17 LET YOUR LIGHT SHINE.

Matthew 5:16

Let your light shine before others, that they may see your good deeds and glorify your Father in heaven.

—MATTHEW 5:16

Have you ever seen a big city at night? The lights are beautiful, aren't they? The whole skyline glitters in the dark.

Jesus told his disciples, "You are the light of the world" (Matthew 5:14). He compared them to the radiance of a town on a hill. Then he said, "You need to let your light shine so everyone can see it. When people notice all the good things you do, they'll start believing in God and praising him."

If you're a Christian, you are meant to be a beacon for this planet. God wants you to shine as bright as a city at night so you'll inspire others to have faith in him.

How? Is shining your light just a matter of doing good deeds now and then, like holding doors for people or returning a lost wallet? These kinds of actions do matter a lot. But there's more to it than that.

Jesus also said *he* was the light of the world (John 8:12). So the light we're supposed to shine doesn't come from us. We

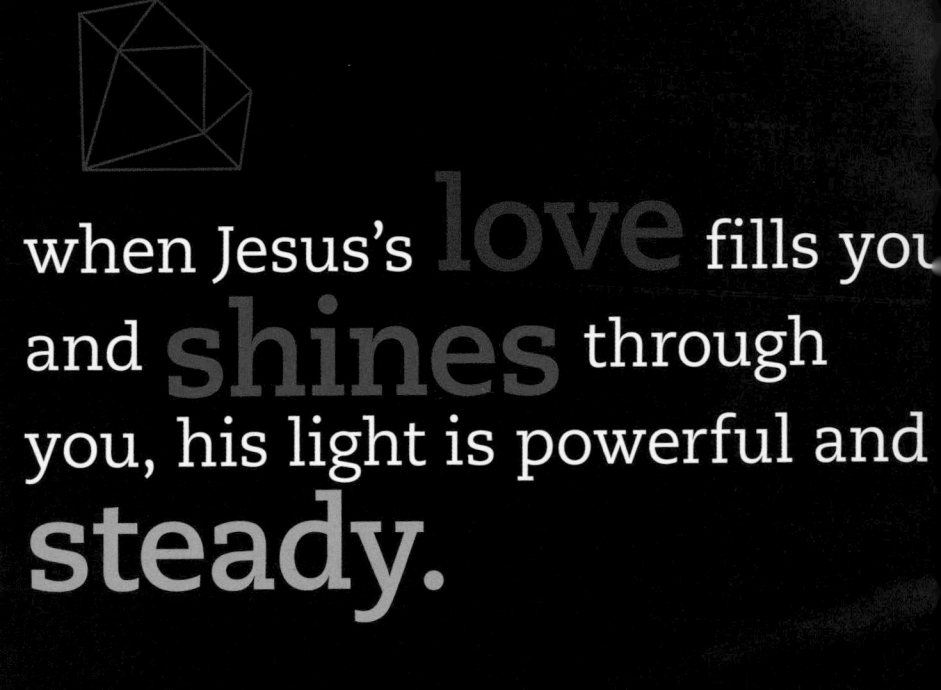

when Jesus's love fills you and shines through you, his light is powerful and steady.

don't have to generate it ourselves like fireflies do. It's really the light of Jesus in us, shining through us.

If you try to shine without Jesus's help, your light will be weak. Sometimes it will go dim, sometimes it'll flicker, and sometimes it'll go out. One day, you might feel like doing good deeds and treating people nicely. The next day, you might help someone but do it with a bad attitude. Another day, you might not bother to help at all. The problem is, a weak, flickering light isn't very inspiring. It won't lead people to God.

But when Jesus's love fills you and shines through you, his

light is powerful and steady. Christ's love compels you to do more than just occasional good deeds. It moves you to care deeply for others every day, show them compassion, and love them the way he does. That's when people see the Light of the World—when they see Jesus in you.

Are you willing to be a beacon for God? Remember, you don't have to generate your own light. The light already exists. It's strong and stable and amazingly bright. All you have to do is let it fill your heart and shine through you so everyone can see it.

MORE GEMS

Be rich in good deeds.
—1 TIMOTHY 6:18

Arise, shine.
—ISAIAH 60:1

18 BE TRANSFORMED.

Romans 12:2

Do not conform to the pattern of this world, but be transformed by the renewing of your mind. Then you will be able to test and approve what God's will is—his good, pleasing and perfect will.

—ROMANS 12:2

Jonah was a prophet who didn't want to do what God told him to do. God said, "Go to the city of Nineveh and warn them to stop sinning." But instead of obeying, Jonah hopped on a ship heading the other way.

Then some amazing things happened to Jonah.

First, God sent a raging storm. The wind and waves battered the ship. All the sailors thought the ship would sink.

Next, the sailors threw Jonah into the water, and the storm died down. The sailors didn't want to hurt Jonah. But he told them the storm was his fault and tossing him overboard was their only chance to survive.

Then a giant fish swallowed Jonah. God sent it to save Jonah's life. Jonah lived in its belly for three days and nights, until finally the fish spit up Jonah onto dry land.

At this point, we're only halfway through the story, and

we've already heard some pretty wild stuff. But now comes the good part.

An entire city was transformed!

Think about that for a minute. Nineveh was so big that it took Jonah three days to walk through it and deliver God's warning.

Jonah told everyone in the city that, because they were so wicked, God was going to destroy them all. The whole city repented! More than 120,000 people lived there. And all of them—from the street sweeper to the king—stopped eating and drinking, put on scratchy old sackcloth, and begged God to forgive them. They gave up their violent, evil ways and decided to start living by God's ways.

They changed their thinking, and their new mind-set changed them.

Did the people of Nineveh suddenly become perfect? No. They had a lot of bad habits to overcome. But something was different about them now. They changed their thinking, and their new mind-set changed them. Before, they were a bunch of wicked sinners who didn't care about God or what was right and wrong. They just did whatever they wanted to do. Now they were trying their best to understand God's will and obey it.

Lots of people today are living like the Ninevites were. That's the general pattern of the world—ignore God, don't worry about what's right and wrong, and do whatever you like. But the Bible warns against living this way. It says, "Do not follow the crowd in doing wrong" (Exodus 23:2). God offers a much better way to live. He wants people to pay attention to what he says, learn what pleases him, and then do that.

You don't have to be perfect to start pleasing God. But you do need to make that important first choice to follow his ways instead of the ways of the world.

It all begins with the way you think. If you line up your thoughts with God's thoughts, God will show you how wonderful his plans for you are. He'll also help you fulfill them. Then something amazing will happen in *your* life. You'll be transformed!

MORE GEMS

Do not follow the crowd.
—EXODUS 23:2

Turn to the LORD.
—ISAIAH 55:7

19 MAKE NOBLE PLANS.

Isaiah 32:8

Scoundrels use wicked methods,
they make up evil schemes. . . .
But the noble make noble plans
and by noble deeds they stand.
—ISAIAH 32:7–8

David decided at an early age to live a noble and honorable life. He chose to trust God and make plans to do what was right. How do we know? Look at the way he acted.

As a young man, David stood up to a giant nobody else was willing to fight. The giant, Goliath, was insulting God and the whole Israelite army. The Israelite soldiers were too scared to battle Goliath. But David knew he served the all-powerful King of Kings. So he pulled out his sling, grabbed some stones, and went out to face the giant. With God's help, David defeated him. (See 1 Samuel 17:1–50.)

Later, David had to deal with another big, bad man. King Saul wasn't as tall as Goliath, but he was taller than everyone else in Israel. Saul had failed to obey God, so God chose David to be the new king. When Saul realized this, he wanted to kill David.

This time, instead of fighting, David fled to the wilderness and hid. That was the noble and honorable thing to do. There was an important difference between Goliath and Saul: Goliath was Israel's enemy; Saul was Israel's king. David knew it wouldn't be right for him to fight Saul.

King Saul and his army kept looking for David. One night, David and one of his friends snuck into the camp of King Saul's army. David's friend wanted to kill Saul, but David

Decide ahead of time
to always trust God and
**do what's
right.**

wouldn't let him. David said, "God will make me king when the time is right." Instead, David took King Saul's spear and water jug so he could later prove to Saul that he wouldn't hurt Saul. (See 1 Samuel 26.) Eventually, God did make David the new king.

David made noble plans. He did what was right, whether that meant standing up and fighting with God's help or treating others honorably while God handled the situation.

You can live nobly and honorably too. What's the secret? Decide ahead of time to always trust God and do what's right. (God will show you what the right thing is.) Ask God today to help you make noble plans and give you the courage and strength to follow them.

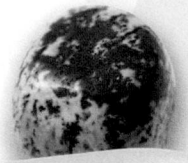

MORE GEMS

Live honorably.
—HEBREWS 13:18

Pursue righteousness.
—PROVERBS 15:9

20 GAIN A HEART OF WISDOM.

Psalm 90:12

Get wisdom.
Though it cost all you have, get understanding.
—PROVERBS 4:7

What are you doing your best to get? Are you finishing all your homework to make good grades? Are you doing extra chores to get money? Are you trying hard to be the best player on your team?

What if God showed up one night and said, "I'll give you whatever you want." What would you ask for?

That's exactly what happened to Solomon. After his father, King David, died, Solomon became the new king of Israel. God appeared to Solomon one night and said he would give Solomon anything he wanted. Solomon could have asked for a big palace with a fancy throne. He could have asked God to make him famous. Or he could have asked God to get rid of all his enemies. But Solomon had something else in mind.

Solomon didn't feel ready to be king. He was young and had no experience. He didn't know how to rule a large nation. So he wanted one thing more than anything else.

"Give me **wisdom,** Lord," Solomon replied, "so I can lead your people."

"Give me wisdom, Lord," Solomon replied, "so I can lead your people."

God was pleased with Solomon's request. He said, "Since this is your heart's desire . . . wisdom and knowledge will be given you. And I will also give you wealth, possessions and honor" (2 Chronicles 1:11–12). Solomon became the wisest man who had ever lived. God gave him great wisdom and—on top of that—made him rich and famous.

Solomon ruled God's people well, and he wrote many wise sayings (see the book of Proverbs). People traveled from all

over the world to hear Solomon speak. Under King Solomon's leadership, the nation of Israel prospered.

Somehow Solomon knew that wisdom was better than anything else he could have wished for. What about you? Do you realize how valuable wisdom is?

Ask God for wisdom, like Solomon did. James 1:5 says that if you do, God will give it to you. How? God will give you wisdom through the Bible as you read it, through his Spirit as you pray, and through your parents, your teachers, and other godly people as you listen to their advice.

Remember this: God didn't just dump a bunch of facts into Solomon's brain and then go away. God became the *source* of Solomon's wisdom. He'll be your ongoing source of wisdom too, if you ask him.

MORE GEMS

Get wisdom, get understanding.
—PROVERBS 4:5

God gives wisdom.
—ECCLESIASTES 2:26

21 DO NOT GIVE UP.

Galatians 6:9

Let us not become weary in doing good, for at the proper time we will reap a harvest if we do not give up.

—GALATIANS 6:9

A movie named *Rudy* is about a guy who dreams of going to his favorite school and playing football on their team. Rudy isn't super smart, he's not very big, and he doesn't have a lot of natural athletic ability. But he manages to make his dream come true, because of one thing—perseverance. Rudy never gives up!

Can you relate to that? Have you ever had to keep trying and trying to become good at something? Maybe you wanted an A in math, and you had to study longer and harder than anyone else. Maybe you wanted to learn a new skill in gymnastics or get a base hit on your Little League team, and you had to keep practicing and practicing.

Did you give up, or did you press on?

If you're a Christian, God has put you on his team. He has suited you up (Ephesians 6:10–17) and sent you onto the field at a crucial time in the game. God has important work

for you to do. He has given you talents and abilities, and he's expecting great things to happen. So trust him, work hard, and keep going no matter what.

The Bible has a lot to say about persistence. For example, 1 Chronicles 28:20 says, "Be strong and courageous, and do the work. Do not be afraid or discouraged." And 2 Chronicles 15:7 says, "Be strong and do not give up, for your work will be rewarded."

God's message to each player on his team is simple: Don't quit!

That's one of the keys to success as a Christian.

Sometimes the raw determination to press on is the only thing that keeps you going. But that doesn't mean you have to do it on your own. Perseverance is linked to faith. The reason you don't quit is because you believe in God's promise that your work for him will matter and

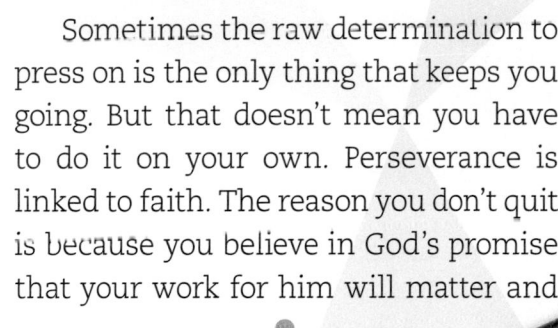

Keep serving
God, trusting him to be with you and help you.

will be rewarded. And you trust God to stay with you through it all, helping you push forward and ultimately succeed.

What good work has God put you on earth to do?

Maybe it's raising money for a good cause, or volunteering to help out at a charity event. Perhaps it's serving at church by performing in a skit for younger children or helping them do a project that teaches them about God's love. It could be doing good deeds for your teachers and classmates at school. Or sharing with the kids in your neighborhood what you know about the Bible and Jesus. It might be as simple—yet powerful—as doing your chores faithfully and cheerfully at home, and treating your siblings with kindness and respect.

Romans 12:11 says, "Never be lacking in zeal, but keep your spiritual fervor, serving the Lord." Whatever God has given you the desire and ability to do for him, give it all you've got! Stick to it, and don't let anything stand in your way. Keep serving God, trusting him to be with you and help you. Your work for God will pay off. People will be blessed, God's kingdom will grow, and God will reward you for everything you do.

MORE GEMS

Do not lose heart.
—2 CORINTHIANS 4:1

Continue to do good.
—1 PETER 4:19

Your work will be rewarded.
—2 CHRONICLES 15:7

22 OVERCOME EVIL WITH GOOD.

Romans 12:21

Do not take revenge. . . .
If your enemy is hungry, feed him;
if he is thirsty, give him something to drink. . . .
Do not be overcome by evil, but overcome evil with
good.

—ROMANS 12:19–21

Do you ever wish you could put on some armor like Iron Man's suit, or grab something for protection like Captain America's shield, or pick up a weapon like Thor's hammer? Sometimes it would be nice to have that kind of power to face the bad guys in this world!

What sort of troublemakers have you been dealing with lately? It's certainly possible to run into a few at school. There can be bullies who hurt kids verbally and physically. And cheaters who copy answers and take credit for other people's work. And thieves who steal things from backpacks and lockers. And liars who make false accusations to teachers and spread rumors.

There can be agitators who disrupt things during class time and start fights after school. And vandals who ruin or destroy things that belong to everyone else. And rebels who defy parents and teachers.

But you don't have to be a superhero to stand up to the evil in this world. You don't need to use force to stop the bad guys. God's Word says that ordinary Christians can overcome evil with good.

There are two main ways to do this. First, do what's right despite what's going on around you and take proper action to stop any wrongdoing you can. That's the way Esther and Mordecai dealt with Haman's evil plot (see the book of Esther). Second, show God's love to the bad guys in your life. That's the way a young Israelite girl who was enslaved in a foreign country dealt with her master (see 2 Kings 5).

Jesus taught some specific ways to love your enemies and overcome evil with good. He said, "Do good to those who hate you, bless those who curse you,

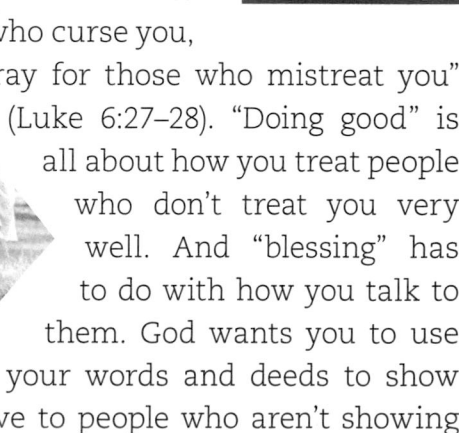

pray for those who mistreat you" (Luke 6:27–28). "Doing good" is all about how you treat people who don't treat you very well. And "blessing" has to do with how you talk to them. God wants you to use your words and deeds to show love to people who aren't showing love to you. He also wants you to pray for them.

The apostle Paul wrote, "Do not repay anyone evil for evil" (Romans 12:17). This is another way to demonstrate love to

"Doing good"

is all about how you treat people who don't treat you very well.

your enemies. Basically, Paul is saying, "Don't try to get even." God doesn't want you to seek revenge if someone does you wrong. Instead, take the hardest step of all when it comes to overcoming evil with good. Forgive the person who hurt you. Reminding believers that God forgave their sins, Paul wrote, "Forgive as the Lord forgave you" (Colossians 3:13).

If you want to defeat evil, then stay loving, positive, and hopeful in the midst of it. Shine brightly in the darkness! When the bad guys see the light of God's goodness in you and sense the hope and joy and peace you have, they may start asking questions. Be ready to share all the reasons why they might want to switch sides.

The best way to overcome evil isn't to go into a rage like the Hulk and try to smash it into oblivion. It's not to fire insults at the bad guys like Hawkeye shooting his arrows. The best way to overcome evil is to win sinners over with love.

MORE GEMS

Love your enemies.
—MATTHEW 5:44

Bless those who curse you.
—LUKE 6:28

Love covers over all wrongs.
—PROVERBS 10:12

23 CLOTHE YOURSELVES WITH HUMILITY.

1 Peter 5:5

Clothe yourselves with humility toward one another, because, "God opposes the proud but shows favor to the humble."

—1 PETER 5:5

How many old sayings can you think of, like "Where there's smoke, there's fire," "Don't count your chickens before they hatch," or "The early bird gets the worm"? Old sayings are often funny ways of giving good advice or pointing out something that's usually true.

Have you ever heard this one: "Pride goes before a fall"? It comes straight from the Bible (see Proverbs 16:18). And it's a good reminder that we are better off when we stop being proud and start being humble.

You've probably heard kids brag about how good they are at skateboarding, then start showing off the tricks they can do. Before you know it, they take a bad tumble. That's kind of what Proverbs 16:18 is talking about. It's a warning that if you let your heart fill up with pride, you're setting yourself up for a fall.

if you let your heart
fill up with **pride**
you're setting
yourself up for a fall.

The apostle Peter compared humility to a piece of clothing. Humility is like a sweatshirt you can put on and take off. So when you're deciding what to wear in the morning, choose to take off pride and put on humility.

What is humility, anyway? Being prideful is thinking you're better than you really are. But having humility, or being humble, is seeing yourself exactly the way you are (no better, no worse)—in other words, the way God sees you. Romans 12:3 says, "Do not think of yourself more highly than you ought, but rather think of yourself with sober judgment." (*Sober* means thoughtful and clear-headed, so in other words, good judgment.)

So what do you look like if you are wearing a sweatshirt with the word *Humble* printed on it? You look like someone who waits your turn and doesn't cut in line, someone who compliments others instead of boasting about yourself, someone who feels good about your accomplishments but doesn't have a big head.

Want to know what else? Read Matthew 11:29, where the Son of God talks about how humble and gentle he is. Then read Matthew 21:1–9, where the King of Kings rides into Jerusalem on a lowly donkey instead of a mighty stallion.

What do you look like when you're dressed in humility? You look like Jesus!

MORE GEMS

Be completely humble and gentle.
—EPHESIANS 4:2

Humility comes before honor.
—PROVERBS 18:12

With humility comes wisdom.
—PROVERBS 11:2

24 REMEMBER THE MIRACLES.

Nehemiah 9:17

Look to the LORD and his strength;
seek his face always.
Remember the wonders he has done,
his miracles, and the judgments he pronounced.
—1 CHRONICLES 16:11–12

It's really cool to stand in the spot where something great happened. Like touring the studio where some of your favorite music was recorded. Or visiting the launch pad where rockets blasted off for the moon. Or walking around the location where a famous movie scene was filmed. Somehow, being there makes what happened seem more real.

Can you imagine what it would be like to see the place where a miracle occurred? Like the Red Sea, where the waters divided so the Israelites could walk through. Or the Jordan River, where the water stopped flowing so God's people could cross. Or Jericho, where the huge city wall came crashing down. Or the Sea of Galilee, where Jesus walked on the waves. Or the mountainside where he fed 5,000 people from one boy's lunch bag.

Maybe you'll get the chance to visit some of these places

one day. That would be awesome! But going there isn't really what matters. What's important is knowing that God has done amazing things.

Learning about God's miracles reminds you how great God is. The more you think about all the wonders he has done, the more you appreciate his wisdom and power. Reflecting on God's miracles builds up your respect and love for him. It inspires you to honor and worship him.

It also builds your trust in him. Just think how many times God rescued his children so faithfully and in such mighty ways, such as making water gush out of a rock so the Israelites wouldn't die of thirst (see Exodus 17), sending an angel to save Daniel from the lions (see Daniel 6), and causing an earthquake to get Paul and Silas out of prison (see Acts 16).

No matter what happens, your almighty Father will be there for you. He can do the impossible!

To remember God's miracles, the Israelites wrote psalms about them (see Psalm 105) and piled up stones as a reminder (see Joshua 4). So what can you do to remember the miracles?

Start by reading about them in the Bible. Then read other books by Christian authors that describe God's miracles. You can also watch movies about them. Christian actors and directors have made wonderful films that show all the drama and excitement of God's amazing deeds.

One of the best ways to remember God's miracles is to

God has been doing **miracles** all through history, and he's still doing them today!

get creative. Make a picture book showing all the miracles from the Bible you can think of. Write a poem or song about "everyday" miracles—like a sunrise, a snowfall, or a flock of birds flying in the shape of a V. Ask godly people you know to tell you about the miracles they've seen God do and record their stories. Put on a skit at home showing some of the miracles *you've* seen God do—such as providing food and clothes for your family or helping someone deal with a tough situation.

After God parted the Red Sea to save his people from the Egyptian army, Moses and the Israelites praised him, singing, "Who is like you—majestic in holiness, awesome in glory, working wonders?" (Exodus 15:11). Never forget God's miraculous deeds. And not just the ones back in Bible times. God has been doing miracles all through history, and he's still doing them today!

MORE GEMS

The LORD is powerful.
—JOSHUA 4:24

He has done marvelous things.
—PSALM 98:1

Remember the wonders.
—1 CHRONICLES 16:12

25 ASK GOD FOR HELP.

1 Timothy 5:5

In my distress I called to the LORD;
I called out to my God.
From his temple he heard my voice;
my cry came to his ears.

—2 SAMUEL 22:7

Jenna was staying overnight at Megan's house. The girls spent the evening running around the neighborhood, enjoying the cool autumn weather. When they got back to Megan's house, Jenna wanted to take a selfie with Megan. She reached into her jacket pocket, but her cell phone was gone!

Megan's family helped Jenna search the home, thinking maybe she left it inside. But the cell phone didn't turn up. "It must be outdoors," Jenna said, trying not to show how upset she was. "It probably fell out of my pocket someplace." But they had no idea where to start looking, and it was too dark to try now.

Megan's dad said, "I'm sure Jenna's worried about this. Let's all take a minute to pray about it." So everyone asked God for help.

The next morning, Megan's dad walked into the kitchen

God will step in and resolve a problem for you if you simply ask.

smiling. Without saying anything, he held up his phone and played a message. Jenna and the others heard a voice saying it was the neighbor across the street. "Good morning! We were raking the leaves in our yard and found a cell phone. Does it belong to anyone there?"

When you have a problem and you're stressed out—whether it's a minor crisis, like losing a cell phone, or something more serious—it's easy to forget to pray. But you'll be amazed at how often God will step in and resolve a problem for you if you simply ask.

Isaiah the prophet reminded the Israelites of God's compassion, saying, "How gracious he will be when you cry for help! As soon as he hears, he will answer you" (Isaiah 30:19).

Keep one thing in mind, though. The Bible says, "The Lord is my helper" (Hebrews 13:6), but God isn't like your waiter at a restaurant. He's your heavenly Father. Sometimes he chooses to help in a way you might not understand. Knowing what's best for you, he may do something unexpected. For instance, if you ask God to help you find something,

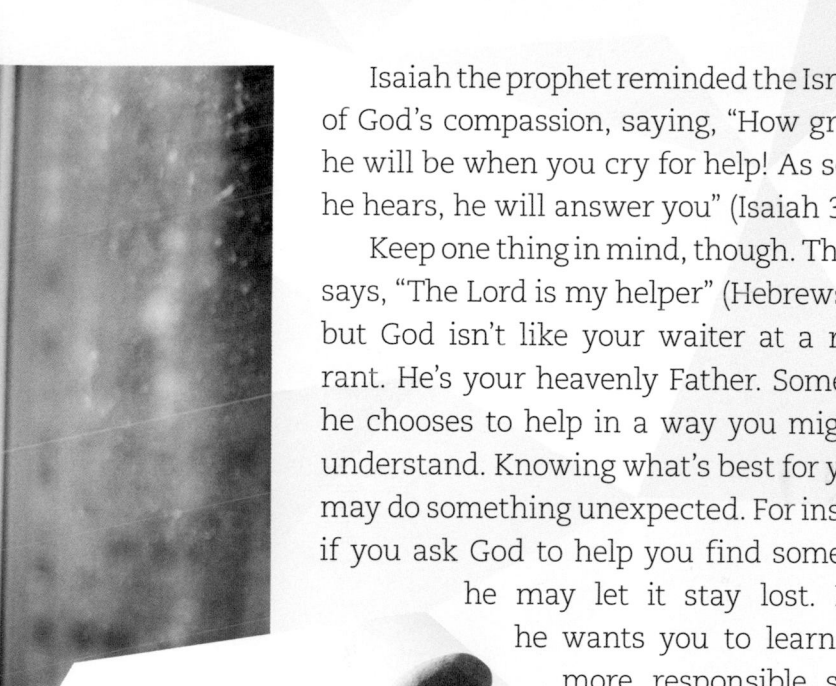

he may let it stay lost. Maybe he wants you to learn to be more responsible so you won't lose something more valuable later. Maybe he wants you to learn to trust him to provide a replacement. Maybe he wants you to realize that you're better off without whatever it is you want back.

God isn't always trying to teach you a lesson in a case like this. He knows what's going on in everyone's life around you, so he may decide it would be better for someone else if he says no to your request. You don't always know what God is up to!

When God doesn't answer your prayer the way you want, he can still help you cope with what happened. He can help you learn what he's trying to teach you, understand why he did what he did, or know how to pray for someone else he may be trying to help.

The next time you start stressing out about something, stop for a moment and pray. Ask God for help. He'll be there for you, and you can trust him to do what's best.

MORE GEMS

Seek help from the LORD.
—2 CHRONICLES 20:4

Cry out to God.
—PSALM 57:2

God will come.
—ISAIAH 35:4

26 ◆ TWO ARE BETTER THAN ONE.

Ecclesiastes 4:9

Two are better than one,
because they have a good return for their labor:
If either of them falls down,
one can help the other up.

—ECCLESIASTES 4:9–10

There's a scene in the Bible (1 Samuel 20) where a young man named Jonathan is practicing his archery skills in a field. Drawing back the string on his bow, he shoots an arrow at a large rock. The arrow whizzes through the air but misses the target completely.

If you were watching this scene in a movie, you might think two things. One, that Jonathan isn't very good with a bow. And two, that he would rather be alone than be on a team, like the archery teams that compete in the Summer Olympics. But you'd be wrong on both counts!

Jonathan missed the rock on purpose. And he did that because he was part of a very special team. He had teamed up with another young man—David, the young shepherd God had chosen to be the next king of Israel. When Jonathan shot his arrow, David was hiding behind the rock. Jonathan shot the arrow the way he did as a signal to warn David that Jonathan's father, King Saul, was trying to kill him. Saul didn't want David to replace him as king.

Jonathan and David both loved God, and they loved each other. So they joined together, swearing an oath of friendship and loyalty. From then on, they would help each other and look out for one another. They would have each other's back.

Christians are meant to be teammates.

This is a great picture of godly friendship. That's what the Bible is talking about when it says, "Two are better than one." You see, being a Christian is really a team event. God wants believers to team up in order to work together, encourage each other, and pray for one another. Christians are meant to be teammates.

Godly friendship can be a team of two, like Jonathan and David. Christians often find one special friend to join with so they can motivate each other to read the Bible and try to live by it. Godly friendship can also be a bigger team, like three or four close friends who talk about God's Word and support one another in their faith.

Are you a team player? Have you linked up with a Christian friend or a group of Christian friends? If not, it's never too late to join God's team. And that's so much better than trying to go it alone.

Christians are stronger together than they could ever be apart. Ecclesiastes 4:12 says, "A cord of three strands is not quickly broken." One strand of fiber by itself will easily snap. But when you braid strands together, you get a strong rope.

That's why you need to be part of a team. Two really is better than one. Three or four is better yet. Don't miss out on all the benefits of being on God's team. Sign up now!

MORE GEMS

Be devoted to one another.
—ROMANS 12:10

Encourage one another daily.
—HEBREWS 3:13

Pray for each other.
—JAMES 5:16

27 COME NEAR TO GOD.

James 4:8

Come near to God and he will come near to you.
—JAMES 4:8

Police officers sometimes ride horses when they're watching over a crowd at a big event like a parade or festival. What do you imagine would happen if you walked up to an officer sitting on a horse and said hello? Would he say, "Go away, I'm busy"? Or would he look down, smile, and take some time to talk? Maybe he would come down to stand next to you so you could pet his horse. It would depend on what kind of person the officer was, wouldn't it?

Some people think God is like an unfriendly police officer. He just sits up there on his throne in heaven, looking down on the earth, judging everybody, and demanding that they respect and obey him. Everyone must worship him—that's it. He doesn't really care about anything else.

But God isn't that way at all. That's why it's so important to read the Bible and find out what he's really like.

Is God a mighty King? Yes! Is he a powerful Judge? Yes! Is it important for you to respect and obey him? Of course! But it's also important to know that God is a loving Father who wants his children to draw close to him. He's like a great King on a magnificent horse who wants his son or daughter to reach up so he can take their hand, pull them up to ride with him, and show them around his kingdom.

Did you know you can discover a lot about God by looking at Jesus? In one story in the Bible, Jesus was outdoors in a crowd. Parents were bringing their young children to him and asking him to pray for them. (See Matthew 19:13–15.) Jesus's disciples thought he was too important and too busy to be bothered with kids. So they told the parents to take their children away.

"No, no!" Jesus said. "Let the children come to me. The kingdom of heaven belongs to them, and to anyone like them." He took the kids in his arms, laid his hands on them, and blessed them.

God is not too busy to spend time with you.

What kind of relationship do you have with God? Maybe you know him a little, but the two of you aren't very close. God loves you deeply. He wants you to come near to him so you can get to know him better.

MORE GEMS

Seek the LORD.
—HOSEA 10:12

Meet with God.
—PSALM 42:2

28 WALK WITH THE WISE.

Proverbs 13:20

Walk with the wise and become wise,
for a companion of fools suffers harm.
—PROVERBS 13:20

When Rehoboam became the king of Israel, he faced a big crisis. The people of Israel were angry. "Your father, King Solomon, made us work too hard and pay too much in taxes!" they complained. "But if you go easier on us, we'll serve you faithfully." King Rehoboam wasn't sure how to answer the people. He needed advice. And he had to choose between two groups of advisors (see 1 Kings 12).

So King Rehoboam told the people he would reply in three days. Then he met with the first group of advisors.

These were the older men who had advised his father during the forty years King Solomon ruled Israel. They were good, wise men, and they gave Rehoboam sensible advice. "Be humble, and do what the people are asking you to do," the men said. "Treat them well, and they'll be your servants forever."

Then King Rehoboam listened to the second group of advisors.

These were the younger men. They were his buddies who had grown up with him. They said, "Don't go easy on the people. You have to show them who's the boss. Tell them, 'If you think my father was tough, just wait! I'll be much harder on you.'"

Rehoboam took the advice of the second group. When he gave his answer to the people, many of them rebelled against him. They chose a different king, and the nation of Israel split into two kingdoms.

Why did King Rehoboam listen to such bad advice? It seems he trusted the younger advisors more, because they were his friends.

Maybe he should have picked wiser friends!

Who do you listen to? Where do you turn for advice?

It's so important to find the right people to be your closest friends, the ones you talk to about everything. If you surround yourself with people who give you good, godly advice, you'll make good, godly choices. Instead of tempting you to go down the wrong path or make selfish choices, wise friends and adults will point you toward the best way. They'll help you gain a heart of wisdom (Psalm 90:12) so you become wise yourself. Being wise means you know the difference between doing good and doing evil, and you're smart enough to do good (see Proverbs 1:1–3).

surround yourself with people who give you good, godly advice.

Think about your friends and ask yourself, "Am I walking with the wise?" If not, ask God to help you find better companions.

And don't stop there. Ask yourself the same question when you turn on the TV or go online. Or when you're searching for a movie to watch, some music to enjoy, or a book or magazine to read. In every case, there are people behind the content you're about to spend time with. Are these people wise? Will they lead you in a direction you want to go? If not, ask God to help you find something better.

Wisdom is contagious; you get it when you walk with the wise. And remember, when you spend time with God through Bible reading and prayer, you're walking with the wisest of them all!

MORE GEMS

The wise prevail.
—PROVERBS 24:5

Your wisdom will reward you.
—PROVERBS 9:12

The wise listen to advice.
—PROVERBS 12:15

29 LIVE AS JESUS DID.

1 John 2:6

What kind of people ought you to be? You ought to live holy and godly lives.

—2 PETER 3:11

A few years ago, many Christians were wearing bracelets with the letters WWJD. These bracelets reminded them to ask themselves, "What would Jesus do?" whenever a tough situation came up. For example, if a girl saw a classmate being bullied, she would look at her bracelet and imagine how Jesus might respond. That would help her decide what to do.

Some people still wear these bracelets today. They inspire followers of Jesus to live like him.

So how did Jesus live?

First of all, Jesus was holy, and he was faithful and obedient to his Father. Jesus never sinned; he always did the right thing. Jesus was also wise; he knew God's Word and listened to God's voice. Jesus was prayerful; he often spent time alone with his Father.

Jesus was loving and compassionate toward people, and he was gracious and forgiving. He was humble and served others instead of forcing them to serve him. Jesus was honest, bold, and courageous; he never shied away from telling the truth. And Jesus was noble and self-sacrificing, giving up his life to save others from sin.

Jesus always kept his purpose in mind. Part of his purpose was to teach people about God's kingdom and tell them the good news that they could join it through faith in him. Another part of Jesus's purpose was to show everyone how to live a holy and godly life.

Read all about the great example Jesus set in the gospels of Matthew, Mark, Luke, and John. Pay attention to how Jesus treated others and lived for God completely. Then come up with your own reminder. Maybe BLC for "Be like Christ"! As you face situations each day, ask yourself, "How can I be like Jesus?" and try to do what he would do. Just as important, pray, "Jesus, help me to live the way you did."

It may seem impossible to follow Jesus's example. We can't be sinless; only he could do that. But God gives believers the strength to do what's right, to be faithful and obedient to him. When they fail, he forgives them and encourages them to keep on trying. You won't be alone as you aim to live like Jesus. He'll be right with you, showing you how.

MORE GEMS

Follow the example of Christ.
—1 CORINTHIANS 11:1

We are like Jesus.
—1 JOHN 4:17

30 ▸ FIGHT THE GOOD FIGHT.

1 Timothy 6:12

Pursue righteousness, godliness, faith, love, endurance and gentleness. Fight the good fight of the faith.

—1 TIMOTHY 6:11–12

Can you imagine if you wandered into the woods where kids were playing paintball, and you didn't know there was a battle going on? It wouldn't be long before you were splattered with paint!

Many people don't realize that this world is a spiritual combat zone. They don't know they have enemies who are out to get them. They are attacked, wounded, and taken prisoner, without ever having a clue about what's happening.

You have to realize that there's a war underway on earth, a huge battle between good and evil. You've got to know who your enemies are and who your allies are, so you can do your part to help the good side win.

So let's break it down. The enemy army consists mostly of Satan and his demons. They're the "fallen angels," the spiritual beings who rebelled against God long ago. They were thrown out of heaven and set up their own kingdom on earth. They

If you believe in Jesus, you too are a member of **God's army.**

hate God's kingdom, and they want to destroy everyone in it. So they whisper lies, tempting kids to do evil, like disobey their parents, cheat on schoolwork, or steal other people's possessions.

God's army consists mostly of the Holy Spirit and the good angels. The Holy Spirit is God himself here in the world with us. (God is way more powerful than Satan. God created Satan, so Satan is no match for God!) The good angels are the spiritual beings who have always stayed loyal to God.

Then there are all the people in the world. God created every person in his own image, and he gave each one the freedom to make choices. Some people choose to listen to Satan and his demons and do evil. Whether these people know it or not, they're helping the enemy army. But others choose to listen to God, believe in Jesus, and become Christians. The Holy Spirit enters them and empowers them to do good. They are soldiers in God's army. The good angels watch over these people and protect them, and God gives them special armor for the battle.

If you believe in Jesus, you too are a member of God's army. Be sure to put on the armor God gave you, which includes the breastplate of righteousness, the helmet of salvation, and the belt of truth. Hold up the shield of faith, strapped to your arm. Use the weapons God put in your hands, which are the sword of the Spirit—that's God's Word—and prayer. (See Ephesians 6:13–18.)

Now you know all about the war on earth, and you'll

recognize the attacks when they come. You understand your enemies more, so they won't surprise you or fool you. And you know who your allies are—the ones you can count on for help as you resist what's wrong and stand up for what's right. You don't have to be afraid, because the powers of good in this world are much stronger than the powers of evil. You're ready to fight the good fight!

MORE GEMS

Fight the battle well.
—1 Timothy 1:18

Resist the devil.
—James 4:7

Stand firm in your faith.
—Isaiah 7:9

31 GOD LOVES A CHEERFUL GIVER.

2 Corinthians 9:7

Each of you should give what you have decided in your heart to give, not reluctantly or under compulsion, for God loves a cheerful giver.

—2 CORINTHIANS 9:7

If you've never tried sushi, it might be hard for you to imagine eating raw fish. Uncooked seafood might not *sound* good. Yet people eat sushi all the time, and they love it. Nobody makes them do it. You see them in Japanese restaurants smiling, talking, and laughing as they enjoy raw tuna and salmon wrapped in seaweed!

Sushi is an acquired taste. Just like many other things, you have to try it—and give yourself time to get used to it—before you'll like it.

So, have you acquired a taste for giving?

For a lot of kids, giving is something their parents make them do. When some kids get their allowance or get paid for doing their chores, Mom and Dad make them give some of it to their church or to a charity that helps people in need.

Giving regularly is a good habit, but there's something special about giving because you want to.

The Bible talks about two kinds of giving: *tithes* and *offerings*. A tithe is a part of any money you earn or receive. Technically, it's 10 percent—one dime out of each dollar—because the word *tithe* means one tenth. Christians give a tithe because God told the Israelites to always give him one-tenth of their wealth, which usually consisted of their animals and crops. God wanted his people to do this as a reminder that everything really belonged to him, and as a way to show that they trusted him to meet their needs.

An offering is a gift beyond a tithe. You get to choose whether to give and how much. Some people give offerings to show God they love him and want to help others. Offerings are usually given at special times or at special events, such as fundraisers.

The most important thing about giving is that God loves cheerful givers. But not because he doesn't like to hear people complain—it's because he knows that when people give joyfully, their hearts are in the right place. They are happily trusting him and generously showing their love for him and for others.

Cheerful givers don't grit their teeth when they give a tithe or grumble when they make an offering—as if someone were forcing them to eat something they didn't want to eat. They give freely. Why? Because they've developed a taste for giving. They've tried it and discovered the joy of it.

The most important thing about giving is that God loves cheerful givers.

And now they enjoy doing it!

Jesus said, "It is more blessed to give than to receive" (Acts 20:35). Maybe to you right now, that doesn't even sound good. Could it really be more fun to give away a dollar than to get one?

Ask God to help you acquire a taste for giving. Then "give" it a try! Start giving a tithe on your own if your parents don't make you do it. Pick an amount of money to give as an offering to something such as your church, a charity, or maybe a family who needs it.

Think about how much God has given you. Think about how much good your gift can do. Think about how much joy your gift can bring. Then just open up your hands and let it go. See how you feel. Try it again. Keep giving so you get used to it. Who knows, you might just like it!

MORE GEMS

The righteous give generously.
—PSALM 37:21

Be generous on every occasion.
—2 CORINTHIANS 9:11

Freely give.
—MATTHEW 10:8

32 DO WHAT IS RIGHT.

Deuteronomy 6:18

Do what is right and good in the LORD's sight, so that it may go well with you.
—DEUTERONOMY 6:18

Great authors like C. S. Lewis weave important themes into their books. For instance, you'll see the theme of temptation in *The Lion, the Witch and the Wardrobe* as you read about how the White Witch entices Edmund with delicious candy. And you'll notice the theme of sin as you read about how Edmund betrays his brother and sisters by joining the White Witch so he can rule with her over the land of Narnia.

Have you ever thought about the themes God wove into the Bible? There are many! Let's look at two of the greatest ones to see how they're connected.

First, there's the theme of *righteousness*—in other words, goodness. A life of righteousness means doing what God says is right and good to do. From the beginning of the Bible to the end, it's clear that God wants people to be righteous. God warned Adam and Eve not to eat the forbidden fruit because he didn't want them to die. Later, God encouraged their son Cain to do good instead of evil. All through the Old Testament,

God told the Israelites he would bless them if they listened to him and did what was right.

Second, there's the theme of *grace*—which has to do with forgiveness. Giving someone grace means forgiving them and blessing them even though they don't deserve it. The Bible makes it clear that God gives people grace when they do wrong but then ask him to forgive them. For example, in Jesus's parable about the prodigal son, the father doesn't punish the sinful young man but throws a party to celebrate that his son came back to him. (See Luke 15:11–32.)

Now, what's the connection between these two themes? How do God's desire for *righteousness* and his willingness to give us *grace* work together? If God keeps letting us off the hook when we sin, won't we just keep on sinning?

The connection is the change that takes place in our hearts. What happens is this: God knows we can't be perfect and live up to his high standard of righteousness. So he offers us grace. When we accept this gift, it fills us with gratitude and changes our hearts. Then we *want* to do right—and we know God will help us do it.

God isn't offering us a free pass so we can go on sinning. He sent Jesus to die on the cross and pay for our sins so that "we might die to sins and live for righteousness" (1 Peter 2:24).

Think about your life for a minute. In what area is it hard

God will give you **grace** and forgive you if you ask him.

for you to be righteous? Are you dishonoring God with the words you use? Are you disobeying your parents? Are you being rude or dishonest with your classmates at school? God will give you grace and forgive you if you ask him. He'll even change your heart and your ways. Tell God you want to please him by doing what's right.

MORE GEMS

Gladly do right.
—Isaiah 64:5

Live for righteousness.
—1 Peter 2:24

33 FORGIVE ONE ANOTHER.

Colossians 3:13

*Bear with each other and forgive one another
if any of you has a grievance against someone.
Forgive as the Lord forgave you.*

—COLOSSIANS 3:13

Did Adam and Eve ever argue?

It kind of makes you wonder. There they were, two perfect people in a perfect environment. Everything was awesome! And they not only lived together; they also worked together. It was Adam's job to take care of their garden home, and it was Eve's job to help him. These two loved each other and got to spend all their time together. What could be better? On the other hand, when two people spend so much time with one another, they're bound to disagree sometimes.

So did Adam and Eve ever fight about anything? What if he stepped on her toes, or she threw a shovelful of dirt on him by mistake?

We can probably assume that if Adam and Eve argued, they did it lovingly. They probably listened politely and spoke respectfully. It's unlikely they started calling each other names. It's hard to imagine them holding grudges. Surely they worked things out peacefully and came up with a solution they both could live with.

But what happened after Adam and Eve ate the forbidden fruit and had to leave paradise? Suddenly, they weren't perfect anymore, and their environment wasn't perfect either. How did they get along then? It must have been a different story.

Here's the point: We're all imperfect people in an imperfect world. You're not perfect, your parents aren't perfect, and your brothers and sisters aren't perfect either. Neither are your teachers or your classmates or people at church or the kids who live in your neighborhood. If we're all going to get along well on this imperfect planet, we have to be willing to forgive one another.

The problem is, ever since Adam and Eve sinned, everyone has had to deal with his or her own sinful nature. So it's harder for us to live in harmony than it was for them in the garden of Eden. It's more difficult to deal with conflict politely and respectfully. It's tougher to admit we're wrong and ask for forgiveness. And it's harder to let go of our anger, forgive each other, and put things behind us.

That's why kids sometimes hold a grudge against a classmate and keep bringing it up when they're talking with their friends. It's also why kids often don't say, "I'm sorry," even when they know they hurt someone else's feelings.

Grace is the only solution to our dilemma. Ephesians 4:2 says, "Be patient, bearing with one another in love." When imperfect people live together, sooner or later they'll have to forgive one another. Even if everyone is trying their best to be good, we're going to disagree sometimes, and we're going to step on each other's toes. So we have to learn to be patient, put up with each other's faults, and let each other off the hook. It's the only way this whole thing will work out.

When imperfect people live together, sooner or later they'll have to **forgive one another.**

Remember that Jesus died for our sins, and God has forgiven us. For those two reasons, we need to forgive one another. It may be difficult, but it's doable, and God will help us do it.

Someday all of us who have put our faith in Jesus will be living together in heaven—perfect people in a perfect environment—and things will be a lot easier. But until then, we'll just have to work a little harder to show each other some grace.

MORE GEMS

Be patient with everyone.
—1 Thessalonians 5:14

Bear with each other.
—Colossians 3:13

Overlook an offense.
—Proverbs 19:11

34 PUT YOUR HOPE IN GOD.

Psalm 42:5

*Those who hope in the LORD
will renew their strength.
They will soar on wings like eagles;
they will run and not grow weary,
they will walk and not be faint.*

—ISAIAH 40:31

Here's the recipe for hope: Start with God's promises, then add faith that God will keep them. The result is unstoppable.

During a famine, a poor widow used this recipe to feed herself and her son. (See 1 Kings 17.) It hadn't rained for a long time, so no crops were growing. The widow and her son had hardly anything left to eat—only a little flour and a bit of olive oil. She knew they couldn't survive much longer.

As she was sadly gathering sticks for a fire, a man called out to her. It was Elijah, one of God's prophets, who had just arrived in town. "Would you please bring me some water and a piece of bread?" he asked.

"I have no bread," the widow replied. "All I have is a handful of flour and some oil. I was getting ready to make one last meal for my son and me."

Elijah told her not to be afraid. "Go and do what you planned," he said. "But first bake a small loaf of bread and bring it to me. If you trust God and do what I ask, he promises you'll have enough flour and oil to last through the famine."

Suddenly, the woman had hope. God had given her a promise, and she believed it. Quickly she hurried home to start the fire. She mixed some flour and oil, kneaded the dough, and baked the bread. The tiny loaf used up her supplies, but she wasn't worried now. She knew God would take care of her. Smiling, she delivered the bread to Elijah.

When the widow returned home, she picked up her flour jar. There was plenty of flour in it! She looked into the oil jug.

There was plenty of olive oil too! She had enough ingredients to bake a good-sized loaf of bread for herself and her son. They ate their meal together joyfully, knowing it wouldn't be their last.

She invited Elijah to stay at her home. Each day, God provided all the food they needed to live. As long as the famine lasted, her jar of flour was always full, and her jug of oil never ran dry.

Sometimes people need hope because they find themselves in a bad situation, and there's no solution in sight. At other times, people put their hope in the wrong place, and they get disappointed. And there are times when people need hope because they're simply feeling down. The most important response in any of these cases is to remember God's promises, such as

- "The LORD will be at your side" (Proverbs 3:26)
- "The LORD will guide you" (Isaiah 58:11)
- "God will meet all your needs" (Philippians 4:19)

And have faith that he will keep them. God will open doors, or he'll make a new door. Here's a great prayer you can say for yourself, or for friends or family members, in times of need:

> "May the God of hope fill you with all joy
> and peace as you trust in him,
> so that you may overflow with hope by the
> power of the Holy Spirit."
> —ROMANS 15:13

Do you see the Gemstone in this prayer? "Trust in him."

MORE GEMS

Always have hope.
—PSALM 71:14

Be joyful in hope.
—ROMANS 12:12

Hope in the LORD.
—ISAIAH 40:31

35 LIVE TOGETHER IN UNITY.

Psalm 133:1

Encourage one another, be of one mind, live in peace. And the God of love and peace will be with you.

—2 CORINTHIANS 13:11

Leah, Kristi, and Carly were looking forward to playing together on the volleyball team in their first year of middle school. They practiced together all summer, pushing each other to improve their skills. Tryouts came around, and they were excited when they all made the team!

During the third game, Leah and Carly both went for the ball and collided. They fell, and Carly broke her arm. All three girls were devastated, but most of all Carly. Volleyball was the only sport she played, and now she was out until next year.

Leah and Kristi decided they couldn't let Carly just stay home to recover. They insisted that she keep coming to practices and games. That way, she could experience the season with them, even if only from the sidelines. Carly was still part of the team, and her friends made sure she felt that way.

Psalm 133:1 says, "How good and pleasant it is when God's

people live together in unity!" The word *unity* means oneness. It's what you have when two or more people work together as a single "unit"—like a team. And being a Christian is like being on a really big team.

It's important for believers to get along with each other, look out for one another, and encourage each other. We need to "make every effort to live in peace with everyone" (Hebrews 12:14). In everything you say and do, remember that you are a teammate.

So when a new kid shows up at your church, for example, do your best to make that person feel welcome. Don't ignore them; talk to them! Ask about their family, their school, and their hobbies. You'll make a new friend—a new teammate, really.

Think of ways you can support and encourage your Christian friends, then put them into practice. (Teammates have to practice together, right?) When you see one of your friends standing for what's right, stand with them. And when one of your friends seems down, say something to encourage them or pray for them. You'll give them a hand up and remind them you're both on the same team.

MORE GEMS

Spur one another on.
—Hebrews 10:24

Keep the unity.
—Ephesians 4:3

36 ◆ WITH MY GOD I CAN.

Psalm 18:29

You, LORD, keep my lamp burning;
my God turns my darkness into light.
With your help I can advance against a troop;
with my God I can scale a wall.
—PSALM 18:28–29

Have you ever been scared to take on a big challenge, and then felt God give you a burst of confidence? Maybe you want to audition for a play at the community theater, or start learning computer animation, or find a way to raise a lot of money for a good cause. At first you might be afraid. You don't know if you could succeed, or if you should even try. But if you let God show you some things about yourself and your circumstances, suddenly you may start thinking, *I can do it. I got this!*

A young man named Gideon had this kind of moment—when he said, "Aha! I see things differently now."

Gideon faced a big challenge, for sure. God had chosen him to rescue the Israelites from a large army that kept invading their country and eating all their crops. Gideon was minding his own business, threshing wheat in a place where the

enemy wouldn't see it. Suddenly, God showed up in the form of an angel and said, "The LORD is with you, mighty warrior" (Judges 6:12). Then he told Gideon to go save his people.

Gideon didn't think of himself as a mighty warrior. He had heard stories of great heroes—people like Joshua and Caleb, who fought bravely and conquered Israel's enemies. Maybe he wished he could be that kind of man. But did he really think he could do it? No. He was scared.

So Gideon hesitated. Instead of obeying right away, he asked for miraculous signs to prove that God was really talking to him and that God would really help him defeat the invaders. God gave Gideon the signs he wanted, and then he did one thing more. He told Gideon that if he was still afraid, he should go spy on the enemy that night.

Gideon and his servant snuck down to the enemy's camp and listened to two soldiers talking. One was describing a weird dream he had about a loaf of bread that rolled into their camp and knocked down the main tent. The other said, "That's the sword of Gideon! God is going to give him victory over us!"

This was Gideon's "Aha!" moment. He realized something amazing. Not only did God think he was a mighty warrior; so did the enemy! They were scared of him. Suddenly, Gideon saw himself differently. He began to think of himself as a mighty warrior too. He believed that with God's help, he could accomplish the mission God had given him.

He believed that with God's help, he could accomplish the mission God had given him.

Later that night, following God's directions, Gideon and his small army sprang a surprise attack on the huge enemy army. God made the enemy soldiers panic and start fighting each other. In the end, Gideon and his companions won.

Gideon's story is encouraging for anyone who needs a little more confidence. It's not about asking God for signs from heaven to give you assurance. It's all about letting God show you who you are, how he has gifted you, and what he is calling you to do. If God has given you a desire to take on a big challenge, try to see yourself the way God sees you and have faith that he will help you. That will give you the confidence you need to do something great.

MORE GEMS

Find strength in God.
—1 Samuel 23:16

The Lord is my helper.
—Hebrews 13:6

The Lord gives victory.
—Psalm 20:6

37 HERE AM I. SEND ME!

Isaiah 6:8

I heard the voice of the Lord saying, "Whom shall I send? And who will go for us?"
And I said, "Here am I. Send me!"
—ISAIAH 6:8

Many Bible heroes didn't exactly jump up waving their arms when God wanted someone to do something. When God ordered Moses to tell Pharaoh to set the Israelites free, Moses replied, "But I'm not a good speaker." When God told Jeremiah he wanted him to be a prophet, Jeremiah said, "But I'm too young! I don't know how to give speeches." Jonah didn't say anything when God told him to go to Nineveh; he just ran the other way.

When God showed himself to Isaiah, Isaiah cried out, "I'm doomed! I'm a sinful man, and I've just seen the Lord!" Isaiah didn't feel worthy to be near God. When Peter first met Jesus, he begged Jesus to leave. He had seen Jesus perform a miracle, and he didn't feel good enough to be around him.

But in every case, God stuck to his plan. God had a mission for each person, and he wouldn't let anything get in the way. Ephesians 2:10 says, "We are God's handiwork, created

You don't have to wait until you're all grown up; you can do **amazing things** for God now.

in Christ Jesus to do good works, which God prepared in advance for us to do." God made all of us with a purpose in mind. He'll give us the wisdom, strength, and courage it takes to do the job he's asking us to do.

So what will your attitude be when God calls you to serve him? Think you're too young to do anything meaningful for God? Think again. The apostle Paul told his assistant, Timothy, "Don't let anyone look down on you because you are young" (1 Timothy 4:12). You don't have to wait until you're all grown up; you can do amazing things for God now. Talk to your parents and teachers about ways you can begin serving him.

God forgave Isaiah's sin so that Isaiah could serve God. And Jesus asked Peter to be his disciple even though Peter felt unworthy. God will help you overcome any sin, fear, or inadequacy you think might disqualify you as his servant.

The only thing it takes to serve God is a willingness to say yes. When God is looking for someone to serve him, respond like Isaiah did the second time. Hold up your hand and reply, "Here I am! I'll do it!"

MORE GEMS

Earnestly serve God.
—ACTS 26:7

I am the Lord's servant.
—LUKE 1:38

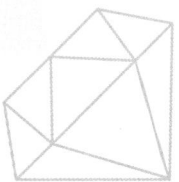

VALUE OTHERS ABOVE YOURSELVES.

Philippians 2:3

Value others above yourselves, not looking to your own interests but each of you to the interests of the others.

—PHILIPPIANS 2:3–4

How would you handle the following situation? You're tired after playing soccer, and you have lots of homework tonight. As you pass the kitchen table, heading for your room, your little sister looks up from the science project she's working on. "Can you help me?" she asks. "This isn't coming out right!"

Do you say, "Sorry, too busy," or do you stop to help?

Jesus told a story about a person who needed help and how other people responded to that need (see Luke 10). In Jesus's tale, a Jewish man was lying beside the road. Thieves had beaten him up, robbed him, and left him there.

A priest came down the road. He noticed the man lying on the ground, but he didn't stop to help. Too busy or something.

Then a Levite came along. (The Levites were the priests'

assistants.) He saw the man next to the road, but he didn't stop either. He was a busy guy! Or something like that.

Finally, a Samaritan showed up. (The Jews and Samaritans hated each other.) He had a lot going on too. But when he saw the injured man, he stopped. Kneeling, he washed and bandaged the man's wounds. Carefully, he put the man on his donkey. Then he took the man to an inn, where he took care of him.

The next day, the Samaritan paid the innkeeper to look after the man. And he promised to pay back the innkeeper for anything else the man might need.

So when someone needs *your* help, do you put his or her needs before your own?

Here's another kind of situation: What if a sibling or friend wants something you want too and there's only one—like the last donut or the video game you both like to play in the car? Do you think of others first?

If you value others above yourself, the way the Samaritan did, you'll be obeying one of the most important commands in the Bible: "Love your neighbor" (Luke 10:27). And you'll become someone who is unselfish, caring, and considerate.

Putting others first is hard to put into practice, but the payoff is worth it. You'll be blessed, and so will everyone around you.

MORE GEMS

Love one another.
—JOHN 13:34

Honor one another above yourselves.
—ROMANS 12:10

39 HONOR YOUR FATHER AND MOTHER.

Ephesians 6:2

Children, obey your parents in the Lord, for this is right. "Honor your father and mother"—which is the first command with a promise—"so that it may go well with you."

—EPHESIANS 6:1–3

Lots of kids dream about what they want to be when they grow up—like a singer, a dancer, a writer, or a movie star. But do you ever think about what you want your life to *be like* when you grow up?

It would be great if your life could be filled with good things, like love and joy and peace, and have none of the bad things, like problems and worries and trouble. That's not really possible because ever since Adam and Eve disobeyed God, the world has been an imperfect place to live. But it is possible to have more goodness in your life. The key to your life going well is to start it right, when you're young—by honoring your mom and dad.

"Honor your father and your mother" is one of the Ten

Commandments. (See Deuteronomy 5, and keep in mind that this includes anyone who is in charge of caring for you, such as grandparents or an aunt or uncle.) This rule is so important because, after all, God gave your parents the job of raising you, and they do so much for you, like providing food and clothes and a house to live in. So they deserve your honor and respect. But the biggest reason to honor your parents is that God says it's right.

So what does it mean to honor your parents? What exactly does God expect you to do?

It's all about showing your mom and dad that you love, respect, value, and appreciate them. This involves the way you think about your parents, how you treat them, and how you talk about them when they're not around.

In God's eyes, when you obey your mother and father, you're obeying him.

One important part of honoring your parents is obeying them. Colossians 3:20 says, "Children, obey your parents in everything, for this pleases the Lord." Doing what your mom and dad tell you to do—promptly, cheerfully, and without complaining—shows that you recognize the authority God gave them over you. In God's eyes, when you obey your mother and father, you're obeying him. And God likes that!

Another big part of honoring you parents is talking to them respectfully. Even when you don't agree with your mom or dad, speak to them in an appropriate way. It's not just the words you say; it's also your tone of voice, the expression on your face, and your body language.

Submitting to your parents is vital too. When your mother and father make a decision—whether it's about a family rule or some request you've made—God requires you to abide by it. It's okay to discuss things respectfully, but when your parents call an end to the discussion, accept their final answer even if you don't like it.

And finally, you honor your mom and dad by listening to their advice. Pay attention to what your parents are teaching you, and then put it into practice. This is one of the ways God gives you wisdom to make good choices: through your parents. And wise choices will definitely help your life go well!

MORE GEMS

Respect your mother and father.
—LEVITICUS 19:3

Obey your parents in everything.
—COLOSSIANS 3:20

 # GUARD YOUR HEART.

Proverbs 4:23

Above all else, guard your heart, for everything you do flows from it.

—PROVERBS 4:23

How do you protect valuable things like your tablet computer or your video games? Do you keep track of them so they don't get stolen or lost? Do you make sure they don't get dirty or wet? Do you handle them carefully so they don't get broken? Do you try not to leave them in the car so they don't bake in the summer or freeze in the winter?

Maybe you take good care of your belongings. Or maybe you don't, and just kind of hope they'll be okay. But what about the things that really matter? What about the one thing that matters most—your heart?

The Bible says protecting your heart should be your top priority. We're not talking about the little muscle that beats in your chest (although it's a good idea to take care of that too). We're talking about your core being—the inner, central part of who you are. Everything you say and do starts there.

If your heart is good, good things will come out of you. If your heart is bad, bad things will come out (see Luke 6:45).

Guard your **heart,**
and good things
will flow from you.

That's why guarding your heart—keeping it good—needs to be number one on your to-do list.

Think of the story of Noah's ark. Do you know what the difference was between Noah and all the other people in the world? Their hearts! When God looked at all those other people, he saw that "every inclination of the thoughts of the human heart was only evil all the time" (Genesis 6:5). But when God looked at Noah, he saw a man with a good heart.

If anyone ever needed to guard his heart, it was Noah. Nobody else was obeying God's commands. Everyone around Noah did whatever he or she wanted to do, with no thought of what was right and wrong. There was so much sin that God decided to destroy the whole world with a flood and start over. But God saved Noah and his family from the flood, because Noah was a righteous man.

How did Noah protect his heart? He did three things:

1. He walked with God.
2. He listened to God.
3. He obeyed God.

God will help you guard your heart like Noah did. That's why it's important to walk with God. In other words, get to know God well by learning all you can about him in the Bible, spending time with him in prayer, and staying close to him every day. Listen to what God is telling you—through his Word and through his Spirit. Find out what pleases God, and then do those things.

Don't listen to anything Satan whispers in your ear. Protect your heart from his temptations and lies. Keep your ears tuned in to God's voice, and you'll keep your heart in good shape.

Guard your heart, and good things will flow from you. The words you say will encourage people, and the deeds you do will bring them joy. And as you bless others, God's blessings will flow back to you.

MORE GEMS

The LORD searches every heart.
—I CHRONICLES 28:9

Be on your guard.
—I CORINTHIANS 16:13

Be alert.
—I PETER 5:8

41 RUN WITH PERSEVERANCE.

Hebrews 12:1

Let us throw off everything that hinders and the sin that so easily entangles. And let us run with perseverance the race marked out for us, fixing our eyes on Jesus.

—Hebrews 12:1–2

Have you ever been in a sack race, where you step into a burlap bag and try to hop faster than anyone else to the finish line? If you think about it, a game like that teaches a good lesson: It's a lot easier to run when nothing is holding you back!

Can you imagine how much easier it would be to win the race if you could throw away the sack? You'd get the prize for sure. In this kind of event, that would be cheating. But in real life, it's not cheating at all. In fact, it's what God says to do.

The apostle Paul describes the Christian life as a race. And like a good coach, Paul offers great advice: "Run in a way that will help you win." (See 1 Corinthians 9:24.)

How? You start by getting rid of anything that will slow you down. Then you keep running and don't quit.

Two kinds of things keep a Christian from running well,

according to Hebrews 12:1–2. There is sin, which entangles you and prevents you from following God. Then there is "everything that hinders." This kind of stuff isn't sinful but somehow distracts you.

For example, how often do you stay up late on Saturday night, watching movies or playing games? Neither activity is wrong, but what if you always wake up Sunday morning tired and grumpy? You drag your feet getting ready for church and argue with your parents. Now no one's in the right mood to worship God. And later you keep zoning out during the service, trying not to fall asleep.

Could it be that staying up late hinders your Christian race? Maybe this habit is like trying to run in a burlap bag. You need to throw it away!

Once you've tossed off whatever keeps you from moving ahead, remember a couple more things. First, you won't get the prize unless you reach the finish line. So don't quit on God! Second, stay focused on Jesus. He'll help you run strong. Don't look at problems, distractions, or temptations to your right or left. Keep your eyes on Jesus, and keep running until you win.

MORE GEMS

Throw off everything that hinders.
—HEBREWS 12:1

Press on toward the goal.
—PHILIPPIANS 3:14

42 SPEAK TRUTHFULLY.

Ephesians 4:25

Each of you must put off falsehood and speak truthfully to your neighbor.
—Ephesians 4:25

Do you know any magic tricks? Can you fool people into thinking you made a quarter disappear or put two halves of a rope back together?

Magicians deceive their audiences all the time with illusions, and all in good fun. But deception is often used to rob others or hurt them. Maybe someone tricked you and took something from you. Maybe one of your friends lied to you and hurt your feelings.

Protecting people from harm is one reason why God insists on honesty. Another is that God's kingdom is filled with truth and light, not lies and darkness. Dishonesty is a hallmark of Satan's realm. Satan is a deceiver, and you don't want to be like him. Jesus said, "There is no truth in him. . . . He is a liar and the father of lies" (John 8:44).

If you lie, you become known as a dishonest person. You actually become a liar. People learn they can't trust you. Then, if you try to tell them about Jesus, they'll find it hard to believe what you say. Being dishonest will hinder you from fulfilling one of your main missions in life. And God has a much better plan for you than that.

As important as it is to speak truthfully, it's just as important to behave honestly. You can deceive someone without lying—for instance, by letting your mom think you're doing your homework in your bedroom even though you're really playing video games.

When you lie, you fool somebody directly; when you behave deceitfully, you fool someone indirectly. Both are wrong. So be honest in word and deed!

Ephesians 4:15 says we should "[speak] the truth in love." That means we should be honest and sincere, and lovingly share the gospel with others. These go hand in hand. If you're honest all the time, others will be more willing to listen when you talk to them about your faith—partly because they can trust what you say, and partly because they're impressed with your character. When Christians show they are truthful, reliable, and honorable, it attracts people to Jesus.

Magic tricks can be exciting. A magician's illusions can be delightful and enchanting. But speaking the truth in love is far more wonderful and powerful.

MORE GEMS

Do not lie.
—COLOSSIANS 3:9

Do not deceive one another.
—LEVITICUS 19:11

Be honest.
—PROVERBS 22:21

43 CHRIST'S LOVE COMPELS US.

2 Corinthians 5:14

Walk in the way of love, just as Christ loved us and gave himself up for us.
—EPHESIANS 5:2

There's something beautiful about a sailboat moving swiftly through the water. Especially with the huge, colorful spinnaker ballooning out front. Seeing the sails so full, and watching the boat skim across the waves so fast, tells you a strong wind is blowing.

A wind like that is a compelling force. If a sailor adjusts his sails to catch it right, the wind will drive his boat forward powerfully. Carried along by such a mighty wind, a sailboat is unstoppable.

What compels *you* in life?

What's the driving force behind the choices you make and the things you do?

Many different things can motivate a person. You can be driven by greed, a hunger for power, an ambition to do great things, a hope to be famous.

For most kids, a major driving force is the desire to be liked. Some kids try hard to be popular, dressing hip and

When Christ's love
truly starts moving you,
it compels you to
love others.

acting cool. Others work at being good in sports to win the respect of their coaches, teammates, and fans. Still others focus on getting good grades, wanting to earn the approval of their teachers and parents.

But there's a much better way to live. You don't have to be driven by the desire for people to like or love you. Instead, you can be driven by love itself! You can set your sails to catch the powerful love God has for you and for others so that it becomes the compelling force in your life.

Sailors have learned how to look for signs that a wind is blowing, and in the same way, you can look for signs of God's love. One big clue that God loves you is that he comes right out and says so. God tells his children, "I have loved you with an everlasting love" (Jeremiah 31:3). And he adds, "Never will I leave you; never will I forsake you" (Hebrews 13:5).

Maybe the best proof that God loves you is what he has done for you. God didn't just say, "I love you." He proved it by becoming a man—Jesus—and dying for you so you could be saved from sin and death. Jesus was able to show you God's love, because he is God. This love is unending, like a mighty wind that never lets up.

So how can you set your sails to catch this strong, steady wind? By reading God's Word, going to church, enjoying Christian movies, books, and music, interacting with other believers, and exploring God's wonderful creation. All this will remind you how much God loves you.

As Christ's love becomes the driving force in your life, ask yourself what it's driving you *toward*. What is it compelling you to do? If you're setting your sails right, the answer will become clear. When Christ's love truly starts moving you, it compels you to love others. You may still wear cool clothes, excel at sports, and study hard at school—but you'll start seeing other people's needs and helping them too. And you'll be doing it all for the right reasons. Instead of grasping for love and acceptance, you'll be giving it away.

MORE GEMS

Love comes from God.
—1 John 4:7

Christ loved us.
—Ephesians 5:2

Walk in love.
—2 John 1:6

44 BEAR FRUIT FOR GOD.

Romans 7:4

*[Jesus said,] "I am the vine; you are the branches.
If you remain in me and I in you, you will bear
much fruit."*

—JOHN 15:5

Every year in the fall, many families like to go apple picking. It's fun to enjoy the cool autumn breeze as you fill your bags with red apples, green ones, or golden-yellow ones—and eat a couple too. Nothing tastes better than a fresh, crisp apple plucked right off the tree.

But in the fall of 2012, people were disappointed when they arrived at their favorite orchards. Instead of seeing trees full of fruit, they saw a sign that said, "We're sorry, there are no apples this year." That spring, the weather had been very hot, and the trees bloomed too early. Then the weather turned colder, and the blossoms froze and died.

Apple growers lost nearly all their crops that year. The story ends well, though. The next year, the harvest was much bigger than normal.

Did you know that you can bear fruit for God, the way a branch on an apple tree produces fruit for its owner?

God is looking for three kinds of fruit from you. The first type is *godly qualities*. They are mentioned in the Bible: "The fruit of the Spirit is love, joy, peace, forbearance [or patience], kindness, goodness, faithfulness, gentleness and self-control" (Galatians 5:22–23).

The second type of fruit is *good works*. These are all the good deeds you do. They are important and valuable! Just remember that good works don't save you from your sins. God saves you by his grace through your faith in Jesus. Then you do the good works God created you to do. (See Ephesians 2:8–10.)

The third kind of fruit is *new believers*. These are the people who believe in God because you tell them about Jesus and show them his love. Jesus told his followers, "Go and make disciples" (Matthew 28:19). When you share the gospel with others, you help them bear fruit for God too.

There's one important thing about being fruitful. Jesus said, "No branch can bear fruit by itself" (John 15:4). A branch will never produce fruit if it's cut off from its source of life and energy. If you want to bear fruit for God, you must stay connected to Jesus. His power, flowing through you, will make you fruitful.

If you want to
bear fruit
for God, you must stay
connected to Jesus.

MORE GEMS

Go and bear fruit.
—John 15:16

Produce a crop.
—Luke 8:15

45 LOOK STRAIGHT AHEAD.

Proverbs 4:25

Let your eyes look straight ahead;
fix your gaze directly before you.
Give careful thought to the paths for your feet
and be steadfast in all your ways.
—PROVERBS 4:25–26

Have you ever headed toward your bedroom to do homework but ended up in the living room, watching TV? You got sidetracked! Like a train switching tracks, you started in one direction and wound up going a different way.

Did you know you can get sidetracked as a Christian? It's possible to begin on the right track and then find yourself traveling down the wrong one. The good news is that only you decide which way to go: onward to your God-given destination or off toward something else.

So keep looking straight ahead. Fix your eyes on Jesus (see Hebrews 12:1–3), and ignore anyone who tries to lead you astray.

In ancient times, when people wanted to go somewhere, they usually walked. So the Bible talks about roads or paths. Proverbs 4:25–27 says, "Give careful thought to the paths for

With the help of God and others, you'll find the **right path** again.

your feet and be steadfast in all your ways. Do not turn to the right or the left; keep your foot from evil." In other words, don't let yourself get *sidepathed*.

It's hard to imagine why anyone would want to leave a perfectly good path and wander off on one that's not so great. But wrong paths don't always start out looking dark and scary. Sometimes they look better than the right one.

That's a good time to check your map. The Bible will remind you, "Be careful to do what the LORD your God has commanded you; do not turn aside to the right or to the left" (Deuteronomy 5:32). Reading God's Word regularly will help you stay on course.

If you ever do take a wrong turn and start feeling lost, stop and pray to God for guidance. Seek advice from your parents or other godly adults. Jeremiah 6:16 says, "Stand at the crossroads and look; ask for the ancient paths, ask where the good way is, and walk in it." With the help of God and others, you'll find the right path again.

Jesus said that the way to everlasting life with God in heaven is like a narrow road, and many people never set foot on it (Matthew 7:13–14). Now that you've found that wonderful road, the last thing in the world you want to do is get sidetracked.

MORE GEMS

Do not turn aside.
—Deuteronomy 5:32

Continue in your faith.
—Colossians 1:23

46 SET AN EXAMPLE.

1 Timothy 4:12

Don't let anyone look down on you because you are young, but set an example for the believers in speech, in conduct, in love, in faith and in purity.
—1 TIMOTHY 4:12

What's the most important word in the Bible? If you had to choose one word to tell someone what the Bible is all about, which word would you pick? There is no right or wrong answer.

Different people could choose different words, because the Bible talks about many important things. But many people might agree on one word as the most important one of all. Let's see if you can guess what it is.

Here are some clues. This word is missing in the sentences below. Can you fill in the blanks? Try to do it without looking up the answer. Read all the sentences before you give up; the same word goes in all the blanks.

"God is _____" (1 John 4:8).
"_____ comes from God" (1 John 4:7).

"Whoever lives in _____ lives in God, and God in them" (1 John 4:16).

Jesus said, "By this everyone will know that you are my disciples, if you _____ one another" (John 13:35).

"_____ the Lord your God with all your heart and with all your soul and with all your mind and with all your strength" (Mark 12:30).

"_____ your neighbor as yourself" (Mark 12:31).

Have you figured it out yet? If not, here's another clue: the answer is in 1 Timothy 4:12, which says, "Don't let anyone look down on you because you are young, but set an example for the believers in speech, in conduct, in love, in faith and in purity."

This word is something every Christian can do. Even young people. That means that if you have faith make a big difference in this world by setting a good example of what being a Christian is all about.

in Jesus, you can do something very important. You can do this one thing to set a good example.

The answer is *love*.

Think about that! Through your example, you can show other Christians how to love God and people, and you can remind other believers how important it is.

You don't have to be a grownup to love. You don't need a college degree to do it, and you don't need an official uniform to do it. With God's help, kids like you can love. Plus you can do the other important things mentioned in 1 Timothy 4:12: talk and act in a godly manner, have faith, and be pure.

In all these ways, you can make a big difference in this world by setting a good example of what being a Christian is all about.

MORE GEMS

Keep on loving one another.
—Hebrews 13:1

Encourage and strengthen
the believers.
—Acts 15:32

47 ALWAYS KEEP ON PRAYING.

Ephesians 6:18

Pray in the Spirit on all occasions with all kinds of prayers and requests. With this in mind, be alert and always keep on praying for all the Lord's people.

—EPHESIANS 6:18

One of Jesus's disciples asked him to teach them how to pray. So Jesus—being the good teacher that he was—gave them a two-part lesson. Just as if they were in a classroom.

First, he taught them a model prayer, which may sound familiar to you. He said, "When you pray, say: 'Father, hallowed be your name, your kingdom come. Give us each day our daily bread. Forgive us our sins, for we also forgive everyone who sins against us. And lead us not into temptation'" (Luke 11:2–4).

Now, if Jesus had drawn a picture of a man praying, what would the picture have looked like? Would it have shown a man on his knees with his hands folded and his head bowed? Or a man banging on someone's door in the middle of the night?

If you picked the second answer, you're right! Because even though Jesus didn't draw a picture for his disciples, he told them a story. And the story was about a man standing in front of his friend's house at midnight, calling out for a favor.

Jesus was teaching his disciples that they should pray boldly, trusting God to give them what they need. In the story, that's what happened. The man's friend got out of bed and gave the man what he requested—because he dared to ask so boldly.

During another "classroom session," Jesus told his disciples a different story about prayer "to show them that they should always pray and not give up" (Luke 18:1). This story featured a widow who kept asking a judge for justice. Someone had wronged her, and she wouldn't stop begging the judge to set things right. Finally, the judge gave the woman what she wanted—because she was so persistent.

Go to your heavenly Father with any problem or need, without fear. He will hear you and answer you. Be confident, because Jesus paid the price for our sins. That makes us righteous in God's eyes and allows us to "approach God's throne of grace with confidence, so that we may receive mercy and find grace to help us in our time of need" (Hebrews 4:16).

MORE GEMS

Devote yourselves to prayer.
—COLOSSIANS 4:2

Pray continually.
—I THESSALONIANS 5:17

Present your requests to God.
—PHILIPPIANS 4:6

48 YOUR SINS ARE FORGIVEN.

Matthew 9:2

Who is a God like you,
who pardons sin and forgives . . . ?
You do not stay angry forever
but delight to show mercy.
You will again have compassion on us;
you will tread our sins underfoot
and hurl all our iniquities into the depths of the sea.
—Micah 7:18–19

Often in movies, people are chased by something evil. They run and hide, but they can't escape the danger. Whatever is after them keeps showing up. They try to fight it off, but they can't defeat it. It keeps coming after them again and again.

Then there's this wonderful moment when their enemy is destroyed. They don't have to run and hide anymore. The monster is gone!

The Israelites celebrated a moment like this after God parted the Red Sea to save them from Pharaoh's army. Moses had told them, "Do not be afraid. . . . The Egyptians you see today you will never see again. The Lord will fight for you"

(Exodus 14:13–14). Sure enough, as soon as the Israelites passed through the waters and reached the other shore, God brought the waters down on the pursuing Egyptian soldiers. When the Israelites turned to look, their enemy had disappeared. Nothing remained but gentle waves on the peaceful sea.

That's what God does to your sin when you put your faith in Jesus. God forgives your sins and throws them into the ocean (see Micah 7:19), never to be thought of again. The Bible says that once God forgives you, he "remembers your sins no more" (Isaiah 43:25). The monster is gone.

Because Jesus died to pay the price for your sins, God has forgotten all about them. You can forget about them too. In God's mind, they no longer exist.

The next time you are by a lake or pond, throw a rock as far as you can out into the water. When the rock vanishes and the ripples subside, thank God that when he forgives your sins, they're gone. Then praise him for saving you from your sin, the way Moses and the Israelites praised God on the shore of the Red Sea.

God is full of joy when anyone turns away from sin and toward him. If you haven't already put your faith in Jesus so that God will forgive and forget your sins, will you put your faith in him today?

God is full of joy when anyone turns away from sin and toward him.

MORE GEMS

In Christ God forgave you.
—Ephesians 4:32

Your guilt is taken away.
—Isaiah 6:7

Christ died for our sins.
—1 Corinthians 15:3

49 REJOICE IN THE LORD ALWAYS.

Philippians 4:4

Rejoice always, pray continually, give thanks in all circumstances; for this is God's will for you in Christ Jesus.

—1 Thessalonians 5:16–18

When you consider all of God's rules—don't do this, don't do that—does it seem like he's no fun? Maybe God is like the Grinch who doesn't want anyone to be happy. Maybe he wants our lives to be dull and gloomy. Or maybe we need to find out what God really wants.

If you were to dig into the Bible to learn about God's will, you might be surprised. For one thing, you'd find some interesting words describing it. In Romans 12:2, the apostle Paul used words like *good*, *pleasing*, and *perfect*. Those don't seem to jive too well with *dull* and *gloomy*.

Time to dig a little deeper.

Next, you'd come across a verse saying that God wants us to rejoice and be thankful all the time. That doesn't sound dull and gloomy at all!

But just to make sure, look up the word *rejoice*. The dictionary says it means "to feel joy or great delight."

God has given us every reason to be **joyful** and **hopeful.**

The more you look, the more you learn. Okay, sure, God wants us to become holy and pray and do good. That sounds a little more serious, but not too bad. Oh, and look: 1 John 2:17 says, "Whoever does the will of God lives forever." Psalm 16:11 adds that when we're with God, he'll fill us with joy, and he'll give us eternal pleasures.

The truth is, God wants nothing but the best for us. And he wants to save us from the worst. We can actually find true joy in him, a happiness that lasts forever. If we walk on the path of righteousness, it "is like the morning sun, shining ever brighter till the full light of day" (Proverbs 4:18). That's certainly the opposite of dull and gloomy. We have all we need right now, thanks to God, and we have a bright future ahead! God has given us every reason to be joyful and hopeful.

When we discover joy in God, it changes our attitude so we can "do everything without grumbling or arguing" (Philippians 2:14). If we do, we'll "shine…like stars in the sky" (v. 15). Who knows? Maybe our joy and hopefulness will rub off on others. It would sure help make the world a happier place.

Is it really possible to go through life joyful and thankful all the time? What about when something sad happens?

Look at the words the prophet Habakkuk wrote during times of trouble:

> Though the fig tree does not bud
> and there are no grapes on the vines,
> though the olive crop fails
> and the fields produce no food,
> though there are no sheep in the pen
> and no cattle in the stalls,
> yet I will rejoice in the LORD,
> I will be joyful in God my Savior.
> —HABAKKUK 3:17–18

Even in trouble, you aren't alone. God is with you. He is still God. And he still loves and cares for you. That brings joy even when you are sad. God knows you're going to feel blue and you're going to grieve sometimes. True joy that only he can give you comes from gratitude for all the blessings you have today and from faith that God will go on blessing you forever.

MORE GEMS

Be thankful.
—HEBREWS 12:28

Be content.
—HEBREWS 13:5

Rejoice today and be glad.
—PSALM 118:24

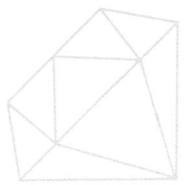

50 TRUST IN GOD'S UNFAILING LOVE.

Psalm 52:8

*I am like an olive tree
flourishing in the house of God;
I trust in God's unfailing love
for ever and ever.*

—PSALM 52:8

Years ago in Tacoma, Washington, a large bridge collapsed. It was a suspension bridge, like the Golden Gate Bridge in San Francisco, California. At the time, it was the third longest suspension bridge in the world. But wind caused it to sway and bounce dangerously. Then the bridge failed, and the road on it fell into the water far below.

Fortunately, there was only one car on the bridge. The driver left it there, because the road was moving so much that he couldn't drive anymore. Walking and crawling, he made it safely to the other side.

Sometimes when you're a kid, life gets crazy. Everything seems about to come crashing down. Maybe something scary happened, or your best friend doesn't want to hang out with

Imagine yourself as
a well-watered tree
sheltered
in God's garden

you anymore. Maybe your parents are fighting a lot, and you're starting to wonder if they'll stay together.

When storm winds blow and you feel unsteady, remember that God loves you and you can trust him. God is steadfast, faithful, and everlasting. He's a strong bridge that won't ever fail.

There were no big steel bridges in ancient times when David wrote Psalm 52, so he used a different way to describe his trust in God. To David, trusting God was like being a tree in God's courtyard—a tree God cared for and treasured. Such a tree depended on God to watch over it, protect it, and give it everything it needed. Then the tree grew healthy and strong.

The prophet Jeremiah wrote something similar:

> Blessed is the one who trusts in the LORD....
> They will be like a tree planted by the water
> that sends out its roots by the stream....
> It has no worries in a year of drought
> and never fails to bear fruit.
> —JEREMIAH 17:7–8

When you're not sure what you can rely on, remember God's love for you and keep trusting him. Picture yourself walking on a mighty bridge that can handle any storm. Imagine yourself as a well-watered tree sheltered in God's garden. God loves you now, and he will love you forever. He'll always be there for you. You can depend on him.

MORE GEMS

Trust in the Lord forever.
—Isaiah 26:4

In God I trust.
—Psalm 56:4

51 ONE PERSON SHARPENS ANOTHER.

Proverbs 27:17

As iron sharpens iron, so one person sharpens another.

—PROVERBS 27:17

Austin and his buds were at the skate park, practicing the tricks they knew. They wanted to make a really cool video to post online and show off their skateboard skills. All of them were competitive; they kept trying to outdo each other by nailing the most difficult moves. Plus, they knew another group of kids who made skateboard videos, and they wanted their video to be better and get more views on the Internet. So they pushed each other to do their very best.

Can you relate? Have you ever engaged in this kind of friendly competition? Maybe you've been in a "sword drill" contest, in which you and your friends flipped through the pages of your Bibles—God's Word, the sword of the Spirit—to see who could look up Scriptures quickest. You may not have realized it, but as you and your buddies pushed each other to think faster, you weren't just "sharpening your swords"—you were sharpening each other!

Christians can sharpen each other the way a honing rod sharpens a kitchen knife. One of the best ways they do this is by helping each other memorize key truths from the Bible.

Before the Israelites entered the Promised Land, Moses told them to remember God's laws. Moses said, "Fix these words . . . in your hearts and minds" (Deuteronomy 11:18). The author of Psalm 119:11 wrote, "I have hidden your word in my heart that I might not sin against you."

When you memorize Scripture, you have God's Word with you wherever you go, ready to use whenever you need it. You can use it to resist the devil's temptations, the way Jesus did in the wilderness (see Matthew 4:1–11). You can tell others about God's promises when they need encouragement. And you can think about those promises when you need some encouragement yourself.

Why don't you and your friends challenge each other to see who can memorize the most Gemstones from this book? Then get together and make up games to see who can say or write down the most Gemstones the fastest. You could use these key truths from God's Word to "sharpen your swords" and sharpen each other.

MORE GEMS

Build each other up.
—1 Thessalonians 5:11

Your commands give me delight.
—Psalm 119:143

Your word is truth.
—John 17:17

52 GLORIFY THE KING OF HEAVEN.

> ### Daniel 4:37
>
> *Praise and exalt and glorify the King of heaven, because everything he does is right and all his ways are just.*
>
> —DANIEL 4:37

Have you ever wanted to honor one of your parents in a special way? Maybe it was your dad's birthday. Or your mom got a promotion at work. Or you gave your pop a "World's Greatest Dad" coffee mug on Father's Day. Maybe you stood in front of your class with your mom or dad on "Take Your Parent to School Day." You told your classmates about how hard they work to feed you, buy you clothes, and get you where you need to go. You bragged about their special talents, like being able to fix broken electronics or cook the best dinners. Whatever the occasion was, you wanted to show how much you love and admire him or her and tell everyone how wonderful your parent is!

That's what it means to "glorify" someone.

There are two parts to it: expressing the respect and

appreciation in your heart, and telling others how great that person is so they can esteem the person too.

As Christians, we glorify God in a similar way. On certain occasions, such as Christmas and Easter, we dress up, decorate our churches and homes, and celebrate with special services and meals. On holidays like those, we make an extra effort to show God how much we worship and adore him. And we try to help others see how awesome he is.

You don't have to wait for big, special occasions to honor someone. You can show your parents how much you love and respect them any day of the year. Likewise, you can express your love and appreciation to God anytime you want. And you don't always have to make grand gestures and fancy speeches. You can glorify your mom or dad with a smile and a hug. You can glorify God with a prayer of praise.

You may not have thought of this, but did you know that you glorify your parents—and God—through obedience? Look for this theme as you read your Bible. You'll see it again and again, all through God's Word. King Solomon talked about it (see Proverbs 10:1), Jesus talked about it (see John 14:15), and the apostle Paul talked about it (see Ephesians 6:1–3). Children bring honor to their parents when they do as they're told, and God's children bring honor to him when they listen and obey.

> Every day, in everything you do, thank God, honor him, and give him glory.

Psalm 145:3 says, "Great is the LORD and most worthy of praise; his greatness no one can fathom." God deserves all the glory you can give. Show him each day, in big ways

and small ways, how much you revere him. Sing his praises at church, worship him with your family at home, tell your friends at school how great he is and how much he means to you.

God is our amazing King—wise, powerful, loving, and good. He is holy and majestic, unchanging and eternal. He's not just the "World's Greatest God"; he's the only God. He made the heavens and the earth and everything in them. There's no one like him! Every day, in everything you do, thank God, honor him, and give him glory.

MORE GEMS

Worship God.
—HEBREWS 12:28

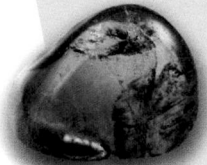

Glorify the LORD.
—PSALM 34:3

Sing praises to our King.
—PSALM 47:6

Live by faith.

—ROMANS 1:17

BIBLE GEMS TO REMEMBER
ILLUSTRATED BIBLE

52 Stories with Easy Bible Memory in 5 Words or Less

Robin Schmitt

Bible Gems to Remember Illustrated Bible, written by Robin Schmitt and illustrated by Kris Aro McLeod, takes children through 52 stories from the Bible. Each includes a powerful gem from Scripture to memorize, a Bible story with colorful and rich illustrations, and more related gems to ponder at the end. God can accomplish amazing things with just a few words. Imagine what he could do in the heart of a person who memorizes and meditates on short "gems" of wisdom from the Bible. Scripture is filled with these "gemstones"—concise statements of five words or less that hold great value, meaning, and power.

Available in stores and online!